Brian Piccolo

A SHORT SEASON

JEANNIE MORRIS

A DELL BOOK

D0052121

Published by
Dell Publishing
a division of
Bantam Doubleday Dell Publishing Group, Inc.
666 Fifth Avenue
New York, New York 10103

ACKNOWLEDGMENT
The people whose names appear in the
text not only were a part of Brian's life
and football career, but also made
substantial contributions to our effort
to tell his story. There are others whose
help also was valuable. They include:
Dr. Douglas Norman, Al Silverman,
Phil O'Hara, Ed Stone, Waltraut Heithus,
Dan and Debbie Boorman, Tim and Holly
Morris, John and Jean Hatteberg, and
Johnny Morris.

ISBN: 0-440-10889-6

Reprinted by arrangement with
Rand McNally & Company
New York, New York 10022
Printed in United States of America
July 1972

30 29 28 27 26 25 24 23 22

KRI

BRIAN PICCOLO: A SHORT SEASON
Beautiful, Full of Guts and Life.
Like Brian Piccolo Himself.

The famous television film **Brian's Song** told the story of a great friendship—the friendship between a black football player, Gale Sayers, and white Brian Piccolo. This book tells more. It tells the whole story of Brian Piccolo's modest life and courageous death.

Gale Sayers said of his roommate: "Pic has the mental attitude that makes me proud to have a friend who spells out the word 'courage' twenty-four hours a day. His spirit could not be destroyed. This was the beautiful nature of Brian Piccolo."

QUANTITY SALES

To Joy, and to Lori, Traci, and Kristi
To Grace, Herb, and Carol
To Irene and Joe, and to Big Ed
To Dan and Mayo, Magic and Ralphie,
    and all the guys
And to George S. Halas

"May all your troubles be *piccolo*"

Brian Piccolo

A SHORT SEASON

Brian Piccolo was a friend and former Chicago Bear teammate who lost a seven-month battle against cancer. Pic was one of those "special" people, a man with solid character and a wholesome sensitivity toward others.

This book was not originally intended to come out in its present form. My wife, Jeannie, and I, like many of our friends, wanted to help Brian and his wife, Joy, in some way during his illness. Joy mentioned that the sheer boredom of the hospital seemed to be one of Brian's biggest problems. Jeannie, thinking about Brian's natural wit and crazy football career, suggested that he write a book. It would give him something to do, to think and talk about. Pic was all for it. His close friend and Bear roommate, Gale Sayers, was about to publish a book and Brian said, "If Magic can do it, so can I."

Jeannie encouraged Pic to put his thoughts and reminiscences on tape. She visited Brian and Joy several times during their long ordeal at Memorial Hospital in New York, and became very involved in Brian's battle.

Brian Piccolo died on June 16, 1970.

Shortly after her husband's death, Joy called and said, "Jeannie, will you finish Brian's book? He would like that."

You won't find much play-by-play football in these pages, at least not in the normal sports biography tradition. Brian and his story offer insights into the lives and careers of the vast number of men who make up pro football's rank and file.

Brian had to overcome many obstacles to achieve success. During his short life he sustained his share of disappointments, but rarely complained.

Pic was a fan's ballplayer, a coach's ballplayer, but above all, a ballplayer's ballplayer.

Brian Piccolo made it to the top at 26.

Johnny Morris

"Man was born to live, to suffer,
and to die, and what befalls him
is a tragic lot. There is no denying
this in the final end. *But we must,*
dear Fox, deny it all along the way."
THOMAS WOLFE
You Can't Go Home Again

Can you believe it, Joy? Can you believe this shit!
Joy's terror-filled eyes met the red-rimmed gaze of
Ed McCaskey across the bed. Even now Brian
wouldn't quit. Even now, after seven months of
hell, he couldn't acknowledge defeat. Three hours
later Brian Piccolo was dead.

When the phone rang in her Atlanta home earlier that evening, Grace Murrath had just tucked
in her three grandchildren, Lori, Traci, and Kristi
Piccolo. The girls and the telephone had become
everything to Grace since Brian and Joy had returned to New York just 13 days ago.

Brian had insisted—no, ordered—Grace to stay
in Atlanta and watch his girls. They would be all
right with "Saint" Grace, the world's greatest
mother-in-law, and he could rest. So Grace sent
her husband, Herb, to New York to be with their
daughter through what they knew would be the
last ordeal. Finally, the call she was waiting for
came through.

"Brian's worse, Mom," Joy said quietly. "He's
restless. The pain is terrible. What am I going to
do? I can't *do* anything."

Grace loved Brian. She remembered a September day in 1958—a Sunday following the first week
of Joy's freshman year at Fort Lauderdale's Central Catholic High School (now called St. Thomas
Aquinas)—when a pudgy, dark-eyed boy pulled
up in front of the house on his motorcycle. He

wore a black leather jacket and moccasins. "Jeepers, Joy," she said, "it's a hood." This was Brian when he was 14 years old. But what Grace now remembered most came later: his smile, his determination, his sweetness, and his loneliness. And his kindness to Carol, Joy's sister.

The phone rang again. "He's better. He's all right," Joy said thinly. "You don't need to come up." She must be in shock, Grace thought. Joy never remembered making that second call.

It had been exactly seven months since the Chicago Bears had played the Falcons in Atlanta.

BRIAN PICCOLO

On the Saturday evening before the Bear-Falcon game, Grace was putting the finishing touches on some of Brian's favorite dishes: baked eggplant and lasagne and, as always, honey cookies. She made an extra batch so he would have some to take back to Chicago. As it turned out, he ate his first cookie with cocktails and the last in a hospital room. But at the moment everything was okay.

Pic often tried to explain southern hospitality to the guys, and now he wanted to show off Grace and Herb and his best girl, Carol; so he brought fullback Ralph Kurek and guard Jim Cadile along for dinner. Brian's folks, Irene and Joseph Piccolo, who had come up from Fort Lauderdale, were staying with the Murraths. This was the first regular season game in which Brian's parents would see him participate—and the last.

Brian, with his usual combination of love and sarcasm, gave Carol one of her more memorable evenings. Carol was 20 years old and severely handicapped by cerebral palsy. She had never known a minute of normalcy. But she had a man in her life—and all the affection, teasing, fun, and love that Brian instinctively knew she craved. He had felt Carol's need from the moment he met her on that Sunday in Fort Lauderdale when she was eight years old. With Brian, Carol felt whole.

It was a happy evening, and Brian's cough didn't alarm the Murraths or the Piccolos. Every winter he had some kind of a cold, which he ignored. And this was November 15th, so the cough seemed natural.

It also seemed natural when Brian left the game the next day. Except for the second half of '68, when Gale Sayers had hurt his knee, Brian had spent his entire professional career running on and off the field. Finally, this season, his fifth, they had let him play with Gale rather than behind him. The coaches had apparently forgotten that he was "too small" and "too slow" and had put him in at fullback. First-stringer Ronnie Bull's bum knee might have had some bearing on the decision, but Pic wouldn't admit it. He felt his time had come. Brian went off the field in the fourth quarter after scoring to make it 31 points for the Bears. But the Falcons scored 48.

What his family could not know was that, for the first time in his career, Brian had taken himself out of a game. He was not able to catch his breath. He had to get to the bench.

My heart hurts, he said.

And it did.

I didn't go back with the club Sunday night after the game. I had to give a speech the next day for the Greenville, South Carolina, Touchdown Club. I like the South. I was born in Pittsfield, Massachusetts, but we moved to Fort Lauderdale when I was three. I guess Pittsfield's about as Yankee as you can get—but my heart's in Dixie.

Anyhow, I couldn't quit coughing. The Greenville guys were pretty good about it, but I felt it was a bad scene. So when I got back to Chicago on Tuesday, I took myself to practice and then right to the hospital. But before I left Wrigley Field I noticed a present in my locker. You'll have to have a little history to get the humor of it.

Ralph Kurek and I used to have an old joke in training camp. The coach always had all of us begin practice with a lap around the field—for Ralphie and me an unnatural act. Magic [Gale Sayers]—he'd take off. Ralphie and I'd plug along together calling that black-assed hot dog every name in the book. But we had this thing. After a few hundred yards our hearts would begin to hurt. And I'd tell Ralphie, "I think I've got cancer of the heart." He'd say, "Try this massage—it always works," and he'd start rubbing his chest.

With this cough, I'd been voicing the old complaint for the past couple of days. So this particular Tuesday morning I found a case of a new soft drink in my locker. The report had just come out that cyclamates caused cancer in rats, and this drink was full of cyclamates. Ralphie just thought he'd cheer me up.

Anyhow, the cough had been around for about three weeks, getting worse. Ed Rozy, our trainer, had been giving me stuff for colds and bronchial problems, but I just kept losing my breath.

At the hospital I looked for Doctor L. L. Braun. Doctor Braun is our team physician. He's small and preoccupied, and with that concave chest he looks like he just escaped from some ward himself. He must be good, because he sure is busy. And as usual, he wasn't in. But I figured he'd want to see a chest X ray, so I went up and got the picture taken. As in most routine chest X rays, they just took a front view. They told me to sit there while it developed. I'd had an okay picture in July at training camp, so I wasn't too worried.

While I was sitting there a gal came in and said, "You'll have to take your shirt off—we're going to take a side view." This was the first inkling I had that there was something on the X ray. We took the side view, and I waited for the pictures, then I took them downstairs. I hung them up and stared at them. There was something wrong. I stared for what seemed like an eternity.

Finally I saw Doctor Kolb (Doctor Louis Kolb is second in command to the Bears' orthopedic man, Doctor Ted Fox), and we looked at the X rays together. I'm no X ray reader, but I could see a shadow in there. I said, "I'm no expert, Doctor, but that's not supposed to be there." "I'm not an alarmist," he told me. "Let's wait and see." But he called Doctor Braun immediately. Braun took one look, and that's when he informed me they'd have to run some tests and I wouldn't be able to play in the Baltimore game.

Wednesday was test day—the first—and God, how I wish it had been the last. For one thing, they went down my throat with a bronchoscope: nothing. So Thursday they made a small incision in my chest, found the tumor, and took a piece of it. They found it was a malignancy called embryonal cell carcinoma. Christ, but they didn't tell me.

Friday they told Joy. When she came up to see me, her eyes were about as big as they could be and very moist. So I assumed that whatever she knew wasn't very good. "Don't cry," I remember telling her. "You gotta bounce up. It's a league rule."

I wanted to know everything, but I was up in the air. I didn't know what the hell was going to happen next. The doctors there wanted to do the surgery the following Tuesday. They had never done an operation just like this, because of the location of the tumor. It's kind of a rare deal. There are only, to my knowledge, some four hundred histories of operations like mine—my first one, that is.

Anyhow, I had a decision to make. And I was in no shape to make a decision. But I had a lot of good advice. Dick Corzatt, my good friend who just happens to be a doctor, got all the heads together, and it looked like there was a choice be-

tween three centers: New Orleans, Houston, and New York. But one name kept turning up: "Edward J. Beattie, New York."

Turns out we had one hell of a time getting hold of him. Turns out he's upstate at a football game. Turns out Beattie's a big football man.

The decision was made, and I had a couple of nice long days to think about it. Monday we'd go to New York.

Meanwhile, I had finally—as the nurses so crudely put it—moved my bowels. You know what a big thing they make of it in the hospital. I kept telling 'em, "How do you expect a good Italian to take a crap if you don't give him any tomato sauce, for crissake? My system craves tomato sauce." Finally I got someone to sneak me a pizza, and everything came out fine.

Then, too, during this time I felt the power and saw the beauty of George Halas. It wasn't the first time—but it was the most important. The Old Man called as soon as he heard about the malignancy. He said I'd get my full contract plus some clauses that depended on my playing. He told me that he had had to go all the way to England to have his hips operated on (Halas had both hips completely rebuilt by surgery at age seventy-three) and that I should get the best—go anywhere and not worry about expenses. The Bears would take care of everything. And they did.

Chicago Bears are always going in and out of Illinois Masonic Hospital (now called Illinois

Masonic Medical Center), but Saturday, November 22nd, saw the greatest invasion in years. Twenty size-extra-large men were stuffed into room 524, passing the Chivas Regal and giving Pic a bad time.

Dick Butkus was the first one through the door. "What's your ass doing in bed, Pic? Out!" Brian got out. Someone else said, "Will you stop that goddamn coughing, Pic, you're driving me up the wall." Bob Wetoska brought him some giant picture playing cards. There were some jokes about which side he should play with, since the backsides of the cards were mostly . . . backsides.

The guys, by and large, were all pretty straight, Brian said later. *You know how it is—when you mention the word 'cancer' everybody starts diggin'. Hell, they didn't know if it was the last time they were going to see me or not, but I knew it wasn't. I've just always had the feeling that my time wasn't here. I've got too many things to do yet. I'm just not ready.*

The jug went around the room again, but Brian wasn't allowed any. He was still standing. Someone sent a nurse out for ice. Howard Mudd had been in Pic's bed, and now it was sagging under Dick Butkus. The party finally broke up when Morey Colleta walked in with Lori, Traci, and Kristi in tow. Morey lives in Brian's neighborhood, and they are old "paisanos." His entrance gave Brian the chance he had been waiting for.

Gentlemen, he announced, *I would like you to meet my personal undertaker.*

Morey and his brother, Mike, own a funeral home.

The guys laughed, but nobody appreciated the remark like Brian. Battle humor had always been his specialty. The Bears filtered out. It was Saturday afternoon and time for "siesta." Tomorrow they faced Baltimore.

The game against the Colts in Wrigley Field on Sunday, November the 23rd, was the tenth game of the '69 season. The books so far recorded eight losses and only one victory for the Bears. The Bears had found some very inventive ways to get to the short end of the final score. Many of the games had been close. As usual, the optimists were citing bad breaks, but the consensus was that the '69 Chicago Bears had a real genius for losing.

Baltimore, though, was always exciting, particularly in the past few years because quarterback Johnny Unitas provided his share of thrills in Wrigley Field. But today Johnny Unitas would be riding the bench, and last year's Most Valuable Player of the NFL, Earl Morrall, would be starting. That was all right with the Bears.

Everyone wanted to win this one, and there was more than the usual amount of sleep lost on Saturday night before the game. The players wanted to take the game ball back to Pic. They were overcome with helplessness, and it was the only thing they knew to give. Besides they knew Pic. They knew he'd be there at Illinois Masonic waiting for that ball. And he'd be damned mad if they didn't show up with it.

The players weren't the only ones losing sleep. Ed McCaskey, along with his wife, Virginia, was still reeling from the shock of Brian's illness. Virginia was formerly Virginia Halas; and after 11 children and 27 years of marriage to the Old Man's only daughter, Ed McCaskey had been persuaded to join the Chicago Bears as vice-president in charge of a million things—including player relations. That was in 1966. Just about the first thing that happened to Ed in his new job was an encounter with Brian Piccolo.

Football players are not noted for their sensitivity, especially toward management personnel. But somehow Brian sensed the awkwardness of Ed's position, coming into the family organization after so many years, and he knew instinctively that Ed needed help. Besides, Brian had met Ed on a few previous occasions and liked him. Ed knew how to live. He had a nose for nonsense and was a true wit. Also, Ed was crazy about Italian food.

As for Ed, he remembered seeing Brian's picture in the paper when he signed with the Bears in '65 and being intrigued with the name "Piccolo." Ed thought, "If this kid is musical, he can make big dough." *Piccolo* is a diminutive in Italian. It means "very small."

Ed McCaskey is an extraordinary man. With his native comic sense, he injected much-needed humor into the staid Bear organization. And too, anyone who accepts a job putting himself between management and the players on a professional football team has to have guts. On one of the first days of Ed's tenure, second-string halfback Piccolo strolled into his office and invited the new vice-president out for a beer. Ed accepted, and the team easily accepted Ed. Ed credits Brian for paving his way with the players.

And now Ed had a new assignment from George Halas: devote as much time as necessary to Brian and Joy. All other duties were secondary.

Over the past two years, Brian and Gale Sayers had become Ed's special friends. And during that long night of November 22nd, when sleep would not come, and the measure of Brian's catastrophe was overwhelming, Ed's young friends were much on his mind. He knew that Brian's illness would deeply affect Gale. He shared the feeling going through many minds: The Bears must beat Baltimore. Brian must have the game ball. And Gale could inspire the team, he thought.

So Ed climbed out of bed and wrote a speech, and the next morning he called George Halas and read the words to him. And the Old Man said "Yes, of course," and called Gale. Gale, who had already been considering something of the sort, said "Yes," in spite of his philosophy that talk did not make leaders in football.

Gale delivered the speech in the locker room on the morning of November 23rd. It was inspiring and moved many of the players, including Gale, to tears. And it moved the team. With eight minutes to go, the Bears had the Colts 21 to 14.

But then Johnny Unitas came off the bench. The old classicist in his high-topped shoes used a formation from which Morrall had been throwing the ball earlier in the game. His receivers were split wide, drawing linebackers back into their pass coverage zones. The Colt linemen succeeded in working the rush to the outside, and Unitas killed the Bears with the draw play. Tom Matte and Terry Cole did most of the work on the Colts' 67-yard drive, with Cole walking through a gaping hole for the tying touchdown.

When the Bears got the ball back, a clipping penalty put them into a second-and-28 situation, and scrambling rookie quarterback Bobby Douglass's pass was intercepted by Colt defender Jerry Logan on the Bears' 40. It didn't take Unitas long to maneuver his team into position for Lou Michaels's 17-yard field goal. The Bears had lost the one they wanted most, 24 to 21.

Brian was listening to the game on the radio. It was, he said, the most frustrating experience of his life. But when the team filed into the room that night—wives, beer, pizza, and all—and Gale apologized for not having the game ball, Brian responded as usual:

For crissake, if you couldn't get me the ball, just give me the cash.

It was something of a farewell party in room 524, and it ran late. A doctor dropped by for evening rounds and found Ed McCaskey in Brian's bed. Ed apologized for substituting without notifying the referee. Brian had slipped up to another floor to visit a little girl who was suffering from a broken neck. The child died a few weeks later.

When the party broke up, Kathy Kurek volunteered to drive Joy home. The Piccolo home at 8900 south in Chicago is a long drive from the North Side's Illinois Masonic. Ralph and Brian were left alone together.

They really didn't know what to say, how to comfort each other. Staff members at the hospital had communicated a sense of unrelieved doom through the grapevine, and Ralph had heard all the rumors. Brian might not survive the original surgery; the thing had grown to the size of an orange and was dangerously close to his heart; the cancer had some sort of congenital connection, which meant it was especially virulent. Ralph and Brian, who had had such great times together, didn't talk much. They sat and watched television. Once an antismoking commercial came up. Brian had never smoked, but he jumped out of bed and flicked the channels saying,

What the hell do they know!

ADMISSION DATE: 11/24/69   PICCOLO, Brian
                                      HOSPITAL #61-54-12

This 26 year old football player entered Memorial Hospital for the first time on 11/24/69 with a mediastinal tumor found by chest X ray and biopsied at the Illinois Masonic Hospital on 11/20/69. He had a negative chest X ray in June [actually it was in July] of

1969. He developed a persistent cough for four weeks, nonproductive, with some left anterior chest pain and some shortness of breath on exertion. A chest X ray taken by Dr. Arthur Haebich at the Illinois Masonic Hospital showed an anterior mediastinal mass presenting on the left side. Bronchoscopy showed bronchial compression but no intrinsic disease. The tumor was biopsied at the Illinois Masonic Hospital and felt to be embryonal cell carcinoma in a teratoma. He elected to come to Memorial Hospital for therapy . . .

My first reaction to Memorial Sloan-Kettering Cancer Center was one of fear. Doctor Beattie had told Ed he would try to get us a room, but he couldn't promise whether it would be private or not. It's almost impossible to get a private room at Memorial.

Ed, Joy, and I walked into the admissions office about two o'clock. We couldn't get admitted until three-thirty, because the guy whose place I was taking was catching a plane, and he wasn't leaving his bed until then. That's how crowded it was.

The room, when I finally got there, had two other beds in it. And that scared me. It wasn't fancy by any stretch of the imagination. But I saw things I'd never seen before in my life. Patients had different kinds of apparatus sticking out. It frightened me a little bit.

Another thing that bothered me was that I couldn't see Doctor Beattie right away. He was in Atlanta delivering a paper to a medical society

*or something. I anticipated meeting him. I knew
they were going to cut on me. I was scared. I was
on the brink of something—and I just didn't know
what to expect.*

Dr. Edward James (Ted) Beattie is an extraordinary man. Chief medical officer and chairman
of the Department of Surgery at Memorial Hospital, he holds one of the most prestigious medical
positions in the world. He has many roles. As the
responsible officer in a great center devoted to
the treatment and cure of cancer, he is a salesman-
politician-fund raiser with all the facts and the per-
suasive charm to deliver his message: beat cancer. As a surgeon, he is skilled in his art and direct
in his attack. His manner with patients is warm
and positive.

Ted Beattie is probably happiest, though, when
he is teaching—sweeping about his domain with
the aspiring young surgeons in whom he invests
a great intelligence and a vast amount of energy.
His personality is reflected in the atmosphere at
Memorial. Everyone—janitors, elevator operators,
nurses—exudes optimism: a little something extra
for the $200-plus per day.

Memorial is expensive. Here every weapon is
brought to bear on the enemy—cancer. War is
being waged, and the hospital is the battleground.
There is never enough time and money; but the
soldiers are tough.

Beattie is tough. He played defensive guard at
Princeton during the Fritz Crisler era. "Football

players make good surgeons," he says. "Surgeons are aggressive, hard-charging guys. Brian and I understood each other right away." Ted Beattie is also a great communicator.

He reminded Joy of Santa Claus.

Doctor Beattie finally got back on Tuesday. And once I met him, I felt so much better—so much more relieved about having the surgery and about getting the whole thing done. I felt like I was putting my life in his hands—and I guess, my destiny—and I felt good about it. He gave me confidence.

And the thing was, he really knew football . . . and anybody who knows football can't be all bad, right? We talked quite a bit of football that first day. Doctor Beattie spent eleven years at Presbyterian-St. Luke's Hospital in Chicago [now called Rush Presbyterian-St. Luke's Medical Center] and he was a real Bear fan. Not the kind who says, "I've had season tickets for thirty years on the fifty-yard line . . ." but the kind who knows the game, who remembers the really fine players like Stan Jones, Rick Casares, Bill George.

Before he left, he warned me that I was going to spend some time going through a rash of tests. He wasn't kidding. Because the surgery was to be Friday, Wednesday and Thursday were test days —which I'd rather forget—but I guess if you could be objective, the tests would be the most interesting part of the whole deal.

They don't leave much alone with this testing.

In my kind of case, they were just sort of using a process of elimination. They had to find out if there was anything else wrong.

They took a lot of Brian's blood, of course, they always do that. The electrocardiogram was the same thing he'd had at training camp every year. Football players can't have bad hearts. The X rays and the urinalysis were all things he'd gone through, routinely, many times. But never so thoroughly. The test that Brian said could only be described as "unreal" was the pulmonary function test.

A bright-eyed little doctor named Charles Lamonte runs the pulmonary function section at Memorial. A complete understanding of a patient's pulmonary, or breathing, functions is important to many forms of diagnosis and treatment. In Brian's case he was scheduled for thoracic surgery. He had a tumor in his chest, and it was important to know if and how the lungs might be affected.

Dr. Lamonte had a real live one working for him—Sandy, a young female technician who looked a bit like Mia Farrow and came on like Vince Lombardi. Sandy studied Brian's chart a few minutes before he was expected. She felt lucky when she discovered that he was a football player. Her boyfriend was a big fan, and she'd have something to talk about to her patient. In Sandy's job, it was important to gain the patient's confidence and to be sensitive and especially attentive to detail. This kind of testing is imprecise, and the degree of success depends, to a large extent, upon the effectiveness of the technician.

As Brian was beginning to expect at Memorial, the pulmonary function section was a clutter of dials and machines—but Sandy was lovely. She was small, not quite as tiny as Joy, but small. Her hair was long and thick and auburn, and her eyes were hazel. The sprinkling of freckles across her nose made her look especially young. She was cute 'til she started the demonstration.

Sandy cuddled up to the machine, covered her pretty mouth with a scuba-diver-type mouthpiece, and put a nose clip to the freckles. Then she started panting—but not like Mia Farrow. Sandy demonstrates every technique with exuberance, because she figures the patients put about 25 percent less effort into the test than she will in the demonstration.

The tests involve various types of breathing into the machine. In addition to the panting and coughing exercises, Brian had to take the deepest breaths possible and then exhale as fast as he could —all the time with Sandy yelling, "More, more," on the intake, screaming "Now!" when she felt he had reached capacity, and then "Faster, faster!" on the exhale. In this way lung capacity and balances can be measured, along with various volumes. Obstructions or narrowing of breathing passages can also be checked.

Before he left, Brian was calling Sandy "Coach."

As a result of the test indications, Dr. Lamonte

felt that Brian was as normal a patient in pulmonary function as he would get. "Minimally abnormal," was the way the doctor put it. And so he asked Brian to participate in a study he was working on with the drug Demerol. Demerol is a common pain-killer which decreases depth and sometimes frequency of breaths. The test involved drawing blood samples after taking the drug under certain variables such as rest, exercise, and breathing pure oxygen.

Brian at first refused to cooperate.

Number one, I'm no hero. Numbers two and three, I don't take drugs, and I hate to work out.

Nevertheless, he was persuaded to contribute to medical science—but not without adding a full share of Piccolo sarcasm. Dr. Lamonte admitted later that the only test in the hospital that might be less pleasant than the pulmonary function routine was the barium enema.

The testing *was* especially significant in Brian's case. He'd guessed right: there was an extra likelihood that something else would be wrong.

The primary tumor with embryonal cell carcinoma usually starts in the testes. The natural progression would take the disease into the abdominal area and then into the chest cavity. But the doctors discovered no tumors in Brian's testicular tissue, and it would have been most unusual for the disease to jump to the chest, skipping the abdomen. Although rare, primary embryonal cell carcinomas do occur in the chest. No ordinary Big C for Pic.

This form of cancer most often victimizes young men. Their first treatment, after the shock of knowing they are diseased, is removal of the involved testis. It was one thing Brian never had to endure.

The theory is that embryonal cell carcinoma arises from the embryonic gonadal column, a chromosomal arrangement which, in the earlier embryonic stage, parallels the cavity that eventually becomes the mediastinum. The mediastinum is the center chest area which contains a wide variety of vital structures, including the heart and great vessels. As the embryo develops, the tissue deploys or is absorbed or both, according to the genetic code, and all gonadal material will be in its proper place. But once in a while, a bit of embryonic tissue is left behind, somewhere in the body, usually in the testes; but in Brian's case, near his heart. In some way that bit of tissue is triggered into activity and becomes a foreign invader. It may be that many people have in their bodies such leftovers which never become active. It may be that cancer cells are common in the human body and that most people have natural immunologic forces which negate them. The researchers are close to breakthroughs on many fronts.

It was Thanksgiving Day, Thursday, November 27th. Brian honestly felt that he had a lot to be thankful for. Not once had anyone heard him say, "Why me?"

What needs to be done, Doctor? he'd ask. *Okay, gorgeous,* he'd tell the nurse. *Let's get to it. Let's get this thing done. I've got to get back in shape.*

On this Thanksgiving, Brian had a special visitor, special to Brian because he liked the way the man ran the National Football League. Pete Rozelle came and spent the afternoon, and Brian and the commissioner watched the Lions-Vikings game on a color television set donated by Brian's good friend, Tucker Frederickson. They had a good time. Rozelle even gave Piccolo his autograph!

That night Dr. Beattie came in for Brian's last briefing before surgery.

He filled me in on everything they were going to do—everything they might have to do. I guess he could tell that I wanted to know, and he let me understand. Some patients don't want to know. They just don't want to be told anything. I felt so much better after he left. I was ready to get the damn thing out.

HOSPITAL COURSE:

. . . . The patient was seen in consultation by Dr. D'Angio, Chairman of the Radiotherapy Department, Dr. Whitmore, Chief of Urology, and Dr. Robert Golbey, Chief of the Solid Tumor Chemotherapy Section in Medicine. Dr. D'Angio felt that surgical excision without radiation therapy was the treatment of choice unless the tumor could not be completely removed. Dr. Whitmore felt that the testes were normal. Dr. Golbey felt that preoperative chemotherapy should be

employed. Accordingly he received 2.5 mg of actinomycin-d intravenously on 11/26/69. He was taken to
the operating room on 11/28/69, and through a com-
bined sternal splitting incision and extension of his
left anterior thoracotomy a large mediastinal tumor
was removed. It was adherent to the lung in the area
where he had previously been biopsied. It was necessary to wedge excise the upper part of the lingula
and lower part of the anterior segment of the left
lung and to block excise the left phrenic nerve along
with the pericardium to which it was intimately adherent. There was one lymph-node located in the an-
terior-superior mediastinum which on frozen section
was positive for embryonal cell carcinoma. The tumor
was completely removed. The chest was thoroughly
irrigated with many liters of water for spillage. Marlex mesh was used to patch the pericardial defect.
He received several doses of a vaccine antipseudo-
monas. His sputum culture contained beta hemolytic
streptococcus, and occasional colonies of staphylo-
coccus for which he was treated with Keflin intravenously. By the 7th day postoperatively he was
afebrile. His chest X ray was clear with slight elevation of the left diaphragm. His incision was healing
well. He was kept on Leukeran 10 mg daily by mouth
and received the second dose of 2.5 mg of actinomycin-d intravenously on 12/8/69. He was discharged
home on 12/10/69, twelve days postoperative. . . .

It was the longest Friday morning of Joy Piccolo's life. Ed McCaskey was there every minute.
Dick Corzatt canceled his own surgery for the day

and came in from Chicago to be near his friends. Joy had been at the hospital early. They'd told her they would be taking Brian up at 7:00 A.M., and she wanted to see him first. But she was cheated; he was gone when she arrived. Perhaps it was so intended.

The operation lasted four and one-half hours. Dr. Beattie said later that Brian had "some" sternum (breastbone) and he'd had to cut through it with the patience of a Michelangelo. "Also," said Beattie, "the kid had muscles on muscles."

Half an hour after completion of surgery, Dr. Beattie was with Joy, explaining everything. He felt that the operation was a success. Every visible bit of tumor had been removed—and some insurance tissue as well. The malignancy had been closer to the size of a grapefruit than an orange.

Dick Corzatt, because he was an M.D., was allowed to accompany Joy into the recovery room. So Dick was a witness to Brian's first words as he struggled out of the anesthetic.

Call Halas, Pic said. *Tell the Old Man I got through another season with my knees.*

Dr. Beattie had mentioned to Joy, without undue emphasis, that one excised lymph-node showed positive for embryonal cell carcinoma. There are hundreds of lymph-nodes in the chest, and it is virtually impossible to remove them all. But it meant the cancer had reached the lymphatic system. The full pathology report later indicated four and perhaps five other types of cells were in the mass.

FINAL DIAGNOSIS:

. . . . Malignant mediastinal teratoma growing predominantly as embryonal [cell] carcinoma with areas of sarcoma, seminoma, squamous carcinoma and a focus suggesting choriocarcinoma. The tumor encroached on the lung superiorly but did not demonstrably invade the lung. . . .

PROGNOSIS:

It is hoped that in this young man with complete surgical excision and with long range chemotherapy the prognosis will be good. He will return to Memorial Hospital in June of 1970 for evaluation concerning his future activity.

DISCHARGE DATE:

December 10, 1969.

God, it's great to be home! Brian must have said
it a dozen times in the first 10 minutes after arriving with Joy at their new home on Hunt Place in
Chicago. It had taken a long time and a big mort-
gage to make it to this house. But the Piccolos
had finally moved in the previous spring, April of
1969.

Most ballplayers live in apartments and take
plenty of time—if they ever do make the decision—
before they move permanently to their team's
city, probably a reflection of the insecurity
of pro football as well as the indecisiveness of
youth. But Brian didn't fit the mold. He planned
to be with the Chicago Bears for some time, and
he planned to make Chicago his permanent home.
Brian had spent his first season as a Bear living
with friends in southwest suburban Palos Park.
Joy was unable to join him in 1965 because, by
the time the final cut had passed and Brian was
sure he had made the team, she was so far ad-
vanced in her first pregnancy that her doctor in
Atlanta insisted she stay put and wait it out at

her parents' home. Brian had picked a small house in the Beverly Hills section of Chicago not far from his first off-season job in real estate. It was a fine little house, but it got very crowded after Kristi came, and before long they moved to the big house in the lush, hilly area of Beverly.

Perched on the top of a little knoll, the home on Hunt Place was Brian's dream house. It had a playroom big enough for a pool table and a downstairs recreation room with a bar. Brian chose heavy oak-and-leather furniture for this, "his" room, and decorated it with his trophies. There was a bedroom for each of his girls. The huge living room had an entire wall of fireplace but, on this December day of his returning, still hardly any furniture.

It was as if they had been gone a year—or a lifetime. It was just beautiful to be home, to have left their grief behind in New York. Friends had come in, cleaned up, and filled the refrigerator. Brian and Joy would have time to relax, catch up on the myriad business details, and answer all the mail—and Grace and Herb would be bringing the girls home for Christmas.

The minute he walked in the door, Brian went to bed. The next day, on orders from his New York chemotherapist, Dr. Robert B. Golbey, he went to Chicago's Presbyterian-St. Luke's Hospital, where Dr. Robert Slayton administered chemotherapy.

I'll tell you about chemotherapy. It was the worst, the thing I hated. They call it medicine, but they ought to think up a stronger name for it. It's really several medicines—chemicals—that work against any cancer cells that Beattie might have missed. The guy in charge of all this at Memorial is a Doctor Golbey. He has a crew cut, and he never smiles. He scared the hell out of me.

You can take this stuff in pill form, or they'll mainline it for you. Either way it makes you very ill and weak. You want to sleep all the time.

I got one injection before the operation, I guess to see if they could see any result. That one didn't affect me like the later shots. I remember feeling a little nauseous, calling the nurse, and going back to sleep. I got my second about a week after surgery. It was worse. Then I got the news: one month of chemotherapy—that's one shot a week and one pill a day—and two months off—for the next three years! That's a whole year's worth of feeling rotten on purpose. It's enough to make you sick.

Like surgery and radiotherapy, chemotherapy makes the patient sick to make him well. So far, cancer demands fire for fire.

Dr. Cornelius P. Rhoads, the first director of Sloan-Kettering Institute, worked with nitrogen mustard at the Army Chemical Warfare Center during World War II. He and his associate, Dr. David Karnofsky, pioneered and established the first comprehensive program of experimental and clinical cancer chemotherapy in the United States.

Chemotherapy is one of those simple-in-theory

but complicated-in-reaction treatments that have great proven value, but whose potential is far from fully exploited. Much of the basic research has been done at Memorial, and Dr. Golbey is far from the burr-headed purveyor of misery Brian liked to describe. However, the doctor admits "the natural position of my face is not a smile." Along with surgery and radiotherapy, Golbey's chemotherapy is the third army employed against cancer. In his office hangs a sign that says, "RELAX." Dr. Golbey hasn't time to read it.

Joy could have given Brian the shots herself. As a registered nurse, she was qualified. But her nursing experience was useless when it came to dealing with her husband.

Those days at home, after the shock of the surgery and before the children arrived from Atlanta, were a relief to Joy. She had time to think. She could do without thinking about the future, but for some reason she kept recalling the past. Most of the immediate past seemed jumbled: just football and babies and talking to Brian on the run.

But those endless sunny days in Fort Lauderdale. Oh God, why didn't I appreciate them more, Joy asked herself.

Brian and Joy had had a crazy sort of courtship. From the time they had both been high school freshmen in Fort Lauderdale, Brian had planned to marry her. That didn't keep other women out of his life, but he never deviated from his plan. All through high school it was the same thing: Brian was just there—watching television with her dad, eating her mom out of house and home, and forcing Joy to lie to get out of dates with him, because Brian as a teenager didn't interest Joy. The unknown, the "older man," was so fascinating—and at the time, Brian was so . . . *known.*

Joy got out her old Central Catholic annuals that first week home to see if she could figure out from whom some of the Florida "get well" mail had come. She ran across the message Brian had written in her senior book in 1961, just before she left for nursing school in Atlanta and he for Wake Forest College:

> *Joy: When I think back on the most wonderful memories I have had in high school the only thing that ever comes into my mind is these three letters: J-O-Y. You have made high school the most wonderful time of my life and I almost hate to see it end mainly because you'll be in Georgia and I'll be in North Carolina, but I guarantee you that I'll soon know Atlanta as well as the palm of my hand. I would also like to say that you maybe caused one or two of our arguments. I hope, Joy, that you don't ever forget the "Prince Charming" that took you to the prom. Joy, I want you to know that everything good I do*

in college is just for you and nobody else. The things that I said I was going to do I really mean. I think that I should warn you that the first time I see you after we've been away you better be prepared to get the life squeezed out of you. May God bless you and keep you in His care always and I hope that all the plans that we (well anyway, I) have made for the future turn out the way they are planned. I love you.

Brian

P.S. Don't forget absence makes the heart grow fonder. Take care of your sweet little sister, too.

Joy turned back to the mail, hundreds of cards and letters from all over the country. It was overwhelming, and Brian insisted that every piece be answered. One card caught her attention. It was homemade and from one of Brian's Italian buddies. It read simply, "MAY ALL YOUR TROUBLES BE 'piccolo.' "

The whole month of December was "not to be believed." The phone and the doorbell rang constantly. Chicago was beginning to repay Brian. For every child who'd collected an autograph, 10 sent homemade get-well cards. He'd made hundreds of public appearances; and, because of his style, his natural empathy, everyone who had ever shaken his hand or had heard him say his common opening line, "I come to you tonight to talk about a subject close to my heart—me"—felt a personal grief.

On December 11th, the Bears organized a press conference in the Piccolo home. It was a hard day. Brian repeated over and over again that he would come back—that he would play again.

When I first came out of the hospital, I said that, because I thought that's what people really wanted to hear, he admitted to *Chicago Today* Sports Editor Rick Talley, *but now I believe it myself.*

I'm confident I'm going to play, he said again. *But if I go back to New York in June and the doctors say, 'Listen, we don't think you should play football,' I'll be damned if I'm going to play football, because it's not the most important thing in the world anymore!*

All of a sudden there were the three most important things in Brian's world: Lori, Traci, and Kristi Piccolo. On the 21st, Herb and Grace and Carol came up from Atlanta, bringing the girls home for Christmas. But on the 22nd, Brian had to take his chemotherapy again, and that put him in bed for the next few days.

Christmas wasn't the rollicking event it had been when the Murraths and Piccolos had been together before. But they were together. The gayest Christmas anyone could remember was the first one that really included Brian. It was in Syracuse, New York, in 1961.

That was where I finally won her over, Brian said later about Joy.

The only thing Syracuse has as far as I know is snow—and Joy's relatives. Joy's got great relatives —starting with Herb and Grace.

Herb is—well, just an easygoing guy. Nothing seems to bother him. He has a tremendous capacity to take things in stride, although he's a very emotional guy too. Joy is just jammed with emotion, and she gets it from both her parents. But Herb is the kind of a guy anybody'd be proud to have as a father—or a father-in-law. We play a lot of golf together. He whips me. Takes it in stride. But I don't.

Grace—she's got to be the most patient woman God ever created. Also, she's Italian, which makes her okay. "D'Alfo" was her maiden name. But Herb and Grace have really been handicapped, having a handicapped daughter. Especially one with cerebral palsy. It's hard, because, you see, Carol's not mentally retarded, she's sharp. When she was fourteen, she knew that's when the other kids were starting to dance. At sixteen other girls were going out in cars. Can you imagine what a child goes through? And, of course, they take it out on the one closest to them, and in her case, it was Grace. Carol's rough sometimes, but by and large she hangs in there pretty good. We can't fault her. We can't know what it would be like to be Carol.

Still, Grace and Herb are captives. They can't

get babysitters. But they stay happy. You just wonder about all the people who have so much less to worry about, but are so much more miserable.

But Syracuse—I got Joy for good in Syracuse. We were off and on—mostly off—all through high school. But I liked her home. Herb and Grace had as much to do with us ending up together as we did. My two older brothers were gone, and my parents worked so hard, I guess the majority of my homelife was down at Joy's in Hollywood [Florida]. I was kind of like a free boarder.

The first year Joy and I were apart I missed her—I missed all of them. So when I got back to Florida from Wake Forest for Christmas vacation, the first thing I did was go down to see Herb and Grace. They were packing to leave for Atlanta to pick up Joy and head north to Syracuse to spend the holidays with Grace's family. I invited myself along. My folks had no serious objections.

Altogether there were some 30 Detors and D'Alfos—a huge congenial Italian family—who gathered regularly for parties over the holidays. Brian loved them, and they returned his affection. They also helped Brian in his campaign for their beautiful little relative.

Joy didn't feel that the trip to Syracuse was so special in her continuing nonromance with Brian. She remembered it as a good time. And she remembered how much her mother's family loved Brian. Piccolo was, in fact, romancing an entire clan. Pic—he said every game has its turning point, and that was the turning point. From winter '61 on, he was sure Joy Murrath was his.

"He always did think he was Don Juan," said Joy.

Syracuse and December of 1961 had been a place and a time of great promise for Brian, because he knew what he wanted and had a plan for getting it. With Joy in the fold, he was halfway home.

But now it was eight years later, December of 1969. Joy belonged to him; many of his dreams had come true. Brian's life was on schedule except for the interruption called cancer.

Still, December was a month of hope. On the 25th Christianity was nineteen hundred and sixty-nine years old and Kristi was one. On the 26th Brian and Joy celebrated their fifth wedding anniversary by going with Gale and Linda Sayers to a party at the home of another friend and Bears teammate, tackle Bob Wetoska. It would be Brian's first visit with many of their friends since surgery.

As he greeted Bob and his wife, Mary Ann, Brian put his friends at ease with his normal perversity, commenting that the Wetoskas should be honored that he, Pic, had decided to celebrate his anniversary in their home. "Figures, you cheap bastard," said Bob. "Won't take your wife out to dinner—come to my place so you can freeload."

Wetoska was a helluva guy.

January 1970. And Brian was back in his old groove. He ordered an Exercycle to rebuild his legs. Brian loved his legs. The strength of his legs had been his pride, as well as his forte in football, and the loss of muscle upset him. He started playing handball with Dick Corzatt. He went back to his stockbrokers desk at Hornblower & Weeks-Hemphill, Noyes (he had earned his broker's license in 1968). He also returned to his old round of public appearances.

One day Traci asked Joy, "Mommy, why do you always sit on the toilet when you talk to Daddy?" "Because that's the only time I can talk to him, baby," Joy answered. "If I sit on the toilet, he can hear me while he's in the shower or running between the bedroom and bathroom getting ready to go out again."

Sundays during the season were so exciting, and the companionship of other team members and their wives so rewarding, that the wild schedule Brian was locked into the year around was almost worth it. The best part of the whole thing was winning—but that happened less than half the time during Brian's years with the Bears. The "high" everyone felt in '68, when they came within one point in one game of winning the Central Division, that feeling was worth working and waiting for. The only bad part of Sunday for Joy was after the games, because Brian was slow—so slow out of the dressing room. Joy might be standing with Linda Sayers in the gloom of a late, losing fall afternoon. Gale would be out of his uniform, into the shower, into his street clothes, grabbing Linda, and off to a warm restaurant, leaving Joy and a few others, always the same ones, to cool their already frozen heels on the icy concrete. Meanwhile, Gale's backup guy, Piccolo, would be sitting in front of his locker, still in his jock and T-shirt—thawing out, resting—thinking. Pic was exhausted when he played, probably because he worked closer to his potential than most men, and depressed when he didn't. Eventually, and sometimes it was dark by then, Brian would come out, and he and Joy would be off to a big evening with their friends.

But there were many evenings that Joy never shared. Brian was a great one for losing himself with the common man—*he* would listen to the *bartender's* troubles. He would stay until the last autograph was signed, and he rarely turned down an invitation for a beer with the president of the local Lions Club after a speech. As far as Joy was concerned, Brian was convivial to a fault.

Joy remembers one evening when she was particularly anxious for Brian to come home. She had something to tell him, and as the hours crept by, she couldn't sleep. Her fury grew—where *was* he? At 3:00 A.M. Brian came strolling in loaded down with groceries. He was elated. He'd been with some Italian vendors down in the wholesale food district on South Water Street. His new friends had deluged him with gifts. Joy melted—she always did. "How could I be mad at him with that grin on his face and a watermelon under his arm?"

Joy's situation was unusual to begin with. Joy and Brian were married in December of 1964; Lori was born in 1965; Traci in 1967; Kristi in 1968. They chose to live on the far South Side of Chicago, an hour from the Loop in rush-hour traffic and even farther from the North Side's Wrigley Field. Brian rarely came home for dinner when he had a public appearance, and he had them often.

Brian liked to take someone along on his junkets. Sometimes it would be Morey Colleta, because Brian thought it was a great touch to introduce his undertaker. On one memorable occasion, Brian invited his attorney.

Brian's lawyer is a man named Irwin Jann. Irwin is roundish, bright-eyed, aggressive, and very successful at the age of 27. Brian met him at a party, liked him immediately, and decided that Irwin would be his lawyer. It didn't seem to matter that Irwin was a criminal lawyer and limited his practice to serving alleged thieves and prostitutes and the like. Brian chose Irwin. Irwin shared his sense of fun.

One afternoon in January, as Brian was cleaning his desk at Hornblower, he picked up the phone and called Irwin, just down La Salle Street, and gave his lawyer his usual line:

Call up your wife, Irwin, let's go zigging and zagging. Bring Sandy.

Sandy is Irwin's partner, a tiny, brilliant Italian, Santo John Volpe.

Brian came blowing into the offices of Volpe and Jann about five o'clock. He was all steamed up and ready for a big night after a big day. He looked well, and Irwin and Sandy were relieved. As they got into the elevator, Brian showed them his new pair of gold cuff links, with the number "41."

Gale gave them to me, he bragged. *Somebody had some number forties made for Gale and that gave him the idea to have these made for me.*

Sandy grabbed both Brian's wrists and took a good long look at the gleaming number "41s."

"That's terrific, Pic," he finally said. "I didn't know they made I.Q. cuff links."

Brian got back at them. But before this happened, Mrs. Jann and Mrs. Volpe both got calls that night from Sandwich, Illinois, a small town about 45 miles southwest of Chicago. Irwin and Sandy would not, they told their wives, be home for dinner. The two men had to sit through a Piccolo speech at a high school athletic awards banquet.

At the outset, just so they would be at ease, Brian introduced them to the audience:

You may have noticed the two gentlemen who came in with me. I never travel without them. Mr. Jann is my lawyer, Mr. Volpe is my probation officer. I hope you will make them feel at home. The Sandwichers were never told another word about Brian's companions. Naturally, the audience wasn't altogether sure what to think. Brian loved it. Irwin and Sandy squirmed a lot.

And then Pic opened with:

I come here tonight to talk to you about my favorite subject—me.

And in the hilarious speech that followed, not a word about Brian Piccolo. Brian never discussed himself in serious conversation. Few people knew his background. He was a very private man.

Louis (*I prefer Luigi*) Brian Piccolo was born in Pittsfield, Massachusetts, on October 31, 1943. At the time, his brother Joe was eight years old and his brother Don was almost two.

Irene Piccolo, his mother, was of German-Hungarian extraction, born in Yonkers, New York. Joseph Piccolo, Sr., was born in Naples, Italy. Brian was very proud of his Italian blood, and at times during his life consciously tried to mold himself to the fun-loving, full-living Italian stereotype he admired.

Joseph Piccolo drove a Greyhound bus for several years before becoming a sort of pioneer in the driving school business in Pittsfield. Every winter, though, he would close up shop for three months and take his family to Fort Lauderdale, Florida, usually returning home just before Easter. But young Don had a rather serious health problem: he would hemorrhage heavily from the nose and mouth. The doctors could not find a cause, and Irene spent many nights worrying that Don might drown in his own blood. One winter, after keeping the boys an extra month in Fort Lauderdale, Irene noticed a big improvement in Don. When she returned to Pittsfield, the doctor decided that the harsh weather in the North might be causing Don's condition. So Irene sold the house and returned to Fort Lauderdale with the boys. Joe, Sr., would join them as soon as he could sell the business. Brian was three years old.

My mother was the dominant factor in my athletic career, because she always wanted me to be the best. When I played Little League baseball, she used to be right behind that screen. I was the catcher, and she was right there in my right ear.

Irene Piccolo has forgotten very little. She recalled:

"Mr. Piccolo got into the driving school business again when we became settled in Fort Lauderdale. But when Brian was young we sold the driving school and opened a sandwich shop. We always went from driving schools to restaurants—that's the way it was.

"When we built this home here, it was Joseph, Jr., and myself who picked out the lot —the neighborhood was not as built up as it is now—it was practically a wilderness. But we wanted a place for the boys to play where they wouldn't be breaking windows and all. So young Joseph and I picked out the lot, and then there was another section that was being built by the same builder in Coral Ridge. To save some money, we picked out a blueprint, the one that suited us. The builder was slow, but the lady we were leasing from was returning from New York and we had to move in. The house had been promised in December and it was February, and so I just told the builder to wind it up—put in the windows and doors. We had to move in—three boys and a dog.

"As I say, Joseph and myself, we did everything, and then when Mr. Piccolo came down he was so displeased. He said, 'You couldn't go out any further, could you?' He wanted to be right in the heart of town."

The Piccolo home in Fort Lauderdale is a flat, white, very "Florida" house. A low porch runs along the front, and the windows are framed with black wrought iron shutters. The circular driveway in front at one time held five autos, one for every member of the family. The ample yard in back is dominated by heavily bearing fruit trees— avocados, oranges, and grapefruit. It is a practical, sturdy structure—a good house in which to raise three boys—if not as close to the "action" as Joseph, Sr., might have liked.

Irene went on:

"My oldest son, Joseph, he's my guide. I think Brian would have been just like him. Don and Brian were only twenty-three months apart. They were very close as youngsters. In Little League baseball, Don was the pitcher and Brian was the catcher. We called Brian 'Little Yogi.' But Don's size was against him, as far as continuing in sports.

"Joseph is seven years older than Don and nine years older than Brian. I never would let Joe participate in sports as a youngster. When he got into high school, he felt terrible, being so far behind the other boys. So when Don and Brian came along, Joe said, 'Mother, don't raise them the way you raised me. Whatever they want to do, let them go out and do it. You can't keep them confined to doing the things that just you want them to do.'

"So whatever they wanted I was one hundred percent in back of them, and I wouldn't hesitate to do everything I could. The sandwich shop closed at six—there was a time here in Fort Lauderdale when everything closed at six, and I went to games all the time. I was the boys' chauffeur.

"I never wanted my boys to work, not

while they attended school. I told them, 'I want you to earn your living the smart way. In other words, go to school.' I didn't want my boys to think they had to make a dollar, go out and kill themselves, and bend down to people. I didn't bring my children up to be laborers. And now, Joe has his government service. And I knew if Brian couldn't get into sports he wouldn't have to drive a truck. I didn't want them to be common laborers, let's put it that way.

"Don and Brian more or less looked to Joe as their big brother, and they preferred to go to him over their father. So the three boys were very close. After Joe went away to Georgetown University, Brian and Don couldn't wait for him to get home. That was when their good times started.

"Joe took them hunting, which, of course, I couldn't do. And Mr. Piccolo wasn't interested in any of that.

"Mr. Piccolo, he made good money all the time. It is a sad thing. Now there are men who are family men who like to be with their families and there are men who are family men who will say, like, 'Here's a nickel, get lost.' They are good providers, but 'Don't bother me.' As for me, I wanted to be with my children, which I was. And once they got married I never interfered—never."

Brian contended that there was nothing much

to remember about his childhood, just sports.

*Even when there was no one to play with, I'd
go out and swing the bat for an hour, or throw the
ball up and catch it with my glove, or throw it
against the wall and field ground balls.*

Brian was a three-sport man: baseball, football,
and basketball, in that order. He planned to play
major league baseball right up until he got the
scholarship to Wake Forest. During his senior
year, center-fielder Piccolo hit .375. But, he figured, if football was giving him a free ride, he
might as well play in the NFL. Never, he claimed,
did he doubt for a moment at any time in his life
that he would be able to make the grade in professional athletics.

Even in high school Brian wasn't a real stand-
out as far as physical equipment goes. He was always a favorite of his coaches, but probably none
of them realized how important they were to him.
George Lowe was Brian's first coach in Little
League, and perhaps Brian glimpsed early that
there would be men outside of his home to whom
he could look for guidance and after whom he
could pattern his life.

*George just impressed me. He didn't come on
strong. So many people who get involved with
kids give it the old 'get one for the Gipper,' the
Knute Rockne crap. Not that it wasn't effective for
Knute and I guess for some kids. But people like
that turn me off the minute they start and that
was true even when I was little. I was influenced*

*by George to the point where I believed in him
and did what he told me.*

Brian felt the same way about his high school
coach, Jim Kurth. Kurth still has the short reddish
hair, the muscled and sport-shirted look that made
him so popular with Brian and his friends. He was
a jock's jock and he was, and still is, proud of his
rapport with his boys.

"You had to have confidence in Brian because
of his great determination—unbelievable determination," Kurth said. "And then, he had good
legs. He was built from the hind end down."

There was, however, a bigger star in the territory: Tucker Frederickson, later a running back
with the New York Giants. When Tucker and
Brian were in high school, all the Catholic kids
from Fort Lauderdale and Hollywood went to
Central Catholic High School in Fort Lauderdale.
The "big" school, though, was South Broward, the
public high school serving Hollywood. Tucker
went to South Broward.

Dan Arnold, who was Brian's closest friend in
high school, claims that "all the girls from Hollywood who attended Central Catholic [and that
included Joy] used to hold it over our heads that
they knew the South Broward guys [and that included Tucker]. They always left the feeling that
we weren't quite as good." Joy knew Tucker
slightly and used to make Brian furious when she
told him, "Tucker is great, so good-looking, but

he's really above me." It would send Brian into a black rage. Nobody was "above" Piccolo's girl.

Memorial Hospital is just a few blocks from Tucker Frederickson's New York apartment. During Brian's various periods of confinement, the Giants' running back was always eager to help. Not the least of his contributions was his color television set, which he trundled over each time Brian came to New York. He visited often.

Brian had starred in Little League baseball, Boy's League football, and had made every local all-star team. At that time, age and weight restrictions were pretty loose, and boys were allowed to go out for any team. Brian, naturally, went out for the best: top limit 12 years and 105 pounds. At age 8, weighing 80 pounds, he was a star pass receiver, and at age 10, Brian and one other boy, Ozzie Polk, were all-stars—the youngest on the squad. *It's not so dangerous when you're all blood and guts,* Brian modestly reflected later.

With both parents working and Joe, who was the steadying influence in his family, off to college, it was a good thing Brian was involved in sports. Coach Kurth maintains that it's not so much athletics, but the group the boy aligns himself with that keeps him straight. "Brian wasn't a mild boy when he was in high school, he was a wild little kid. He had a motorcycle. He had wheels when no one else had wheels, and he made use of them. But every one of the boys he ran with became a success. Dan Arnold was one of the

57-

best—a tall skinny kid—children's dentist now in Fort Lauderdale. Arnold was as determined as Piccolo."

Brian had a boat, then a motorcycle, and then, right before his senior year, his mother bought him a car. Irene saw to it that her sons never lacked the necessities. Dan and Brian used to spend whole days just driving around. "We often went for hours without talking. We didn't need to. We would always be looking for girls, and never once in all the hours we logged cruising can I ever remember picking up any girls."

Of course, Dan wasn't always around. One summer, on Joy's urging (she had to get him out of her hair, she said), Brian got a job driving a doughnut delivery truck in the wee hours. His mother didn't approve, but her discontent was short-lived. Brian was fired when his boss spotted a girl riding with him at six o'clock in the morning. So it was back to his first "home," the Murraths.

Sometimes Brian and Dan would stop at the sandwich shop after practice, just as the Piccolos were closing. Those were memorable times for Dan. It was always the same. The shop had two sides to it: Mrs. Piccolo ran the bar, or short order, side, and Mr. Piccolo ran the delicatessen. Each had a girl helper. And each respected the other's territory. Dan recalled:

"I must say Mrs. Piccolo made a helluva roast beef sandwich. But when the doors closed at six, it was as if someone had fired a starting gun. She'd look at him, and he'd look at her, and the potato chips would start flying. And Brian would just sit there and pretend it wasn't happening. He would ignore the whole scene. But it had to bother him. Occasionally a fight would erupt when customers were still there. Joe and Irene were famous in Fort Lauderdale.

"One night Brian and I were sitting over a sandwich, and Don came in and asked his mother for money so he could go to jai alai. They must have fought for an hour, Mrs. Piccolo yelling that she wasn't going to give him her hard-earned money for gambling, and Don yelling back, and Mr. Piccolo getting into it too. Finally Don talked her into it, and she gave him twenty dollars on one condition: 'Since you're going,' she said, 'put two dollars on the four-seven quinella for me.' Even Brian got a laugh out of that one."

Coach Jim Kurth's high school football teams finished 4-6, 2-6-1, 2-7, and 4-4 during the four years that Brian participated. In fairness, it should be stated that the Central Catholic Raiders played many schools with twice their own student population.

As a freshman, Brian was a bit fat, a little slow. He played offensive tackle at 185, along with another close friend, Bill Salter. He didn't make the halfback spot until his senior year. All through high school Brian was noted for his fine execution: he could block, tackle, run pass patterns, catch the football. He made few mistakes. And he was beautiful in the locker room: The coach had rarely seen his match as a teller of war stories. Brian was a peerless locker-room entertainer.

As a senior, Pic still weighed 185, but he was leaner and meaner. Coach Kurth remembered one game during Brian's last year when he scored the first three times he carried the ball. It was against Norland High School in Miami. Each play was over 50 yards. Brian averaged 10 yards per carry for the day.

Dan Arnold's favorite high school game was against Pompano Beach, which Dan tags "the story of Brian's life." "We started out on the two-yard line and moved the ball ninety-five yards down the field to their three. Brian carried the ball nine out of ten plays. When we came into the huddle, I pinched the quarterback, Bill Zloch, on the ass, and he called my play (I was the other halfback). I'm sorry I did it, I guess. But Pic was getting all the glory anyway, and I just wanted my name in the paper as having scored. Brian never said a thing."

Brian started a pattern in high school that continued throughout his football career. He hated practice. "He was always the last one out," said Kurth. "We had this mark on the asphalt. When I crossed it, everybody was supposed to be off and running. I'd be walking out the door, and Brian would still be putting on his shoes. As I crossed the mark, he'd come flying past me."

Probably Brian's most outstanding characteristic, the thing, along with his sense of humor, that endeared him to so many people was his lack of reverence for position. He had none of his mother's disdain for labor; in fact, he was always drawn to the workingman. Pope and pauper were all the same to Brian. He could enjoy a long conversation with either. He would listen, mostly, and tease a little. Sometimes he would leave them laughing, always he would leave them warmed.

In high school, Dan remembered, Brian never liked the people he was "supposed" to like. "For instance, he really liked the team manager, a fat guy named Keith Carpenter, whom everyone bullied. He took Keith under his wing, became his protector. Brian was completely sincere about it."

One person to whom Brian was devoted and adopted for a lifetime was his young sister-in-law, Carol Murrath. Carol speaks gutturally, forming words with a barely controlled mouth and tongue. Her family can usually translate, but with others she most often communicates by pointing a wavering finger at letters on a special alphabet board. When Joy and Dan and Brian were in high school, Carol used to keep a list of her boyfriends—her top 10. Brian and Dan were usually in the top three. One day when the boys came over they found themselves ninth and tenth. The man who drove the bus to the Cerebral Palsy Center where

Carol went to school was first. The boys gave her hell for that and bullied her into putting them back at the top.

Even as a teen-ager, Brian often took Carol out. Her father would see that she got to basketball and football games, but he balked at rock and roll concerts. Carol would ask Brian, and Brian would find a way to get her through the mobs of teen-agers, wheelchair and all.

One Sunday, Herb, Brian, and Joy took Carol to church. Herb liked to leave early with Carol because he wanted to have her settled before the crowd came. But Brian never hurried—anywhere —and they were late this Sunday. When they were seated they saw that Carol's favorite priest was not in his usual place in the pulpit. Carol was very fond of the monsignor because he spent time talking to her. Another priest made the announcement that the monsignor was visiting a neighboring church for the day; but Carol only heard that her friend had "gone." She went into convulsive hysterics. Herb was petrified with embarrassment. But Brian got right up, lifted Carol into her wheelchair, and wheeled the screaming, flailing child right up the center aisle and out of the church. Herb was again impressed with Brian's maturity.

"Brian was always so good to Carol. I loved him for that. Even when he and Joy were having a fight and weren't speaking, Brian would come over. Maybe he'd take Carol swimming in the pool. She can't go in alone because she can't sit up without support. He was a big shot high school athlete, but he was never, never too busy."

Sure I spent a lot of time at Joy's. And I helped out at the sandwich shop some. I was the kind of student who did enough to get by, but I got along pretty well with the Sisters at Central Catholic.

From the time I was a sophomore in high school, I was pretty much on my own. Don quit school when he was a junior and eventually ended up leaving town. I was the only one left. My folks had the sandwich shop, and that was hard work. They were down there day and night.

My folks weren't strict at all, but I pretty much toed the mark. A close-knit family doesn't always turn out so well. I think being on my own had a hell of a lot to do with my growing up quickly. Either I did it or it didn't get done.

In the long run, God has been good to me, in plain English. He's given me a helluva lot of opportunities and given me the ability to capitalize on those opportunities. I hope my life continues the same, and I hope I can keep it all in the proper perspective.

It was January 1970. Brian was 26 years old. He believed that he had again been blessed and was cured of cancer. And he had just received an invitation to the Astro-jet Golf Tournament in Phoenix, thrown every year by American Airlines for pro athletes. Anybody who wouldn't be happy about an all-expense trip from Chicago to Phoenix in February would have to be nuts.

Before Brian could leave for his desert vacation, before his mind as well as his worn body could rest, there was something he needed to do. The compulsion had been building in him for weeks.

Joy, I've got to write Freddie Steinmark, Brian had said, over and over again. *But I just don't know how to say what I feel.* And he would put off the letter another day.

Brian had received so many letters of sympathy it should have been easy for him to write one. But young Steinmark was too important. Brian felt that cancer had been even crueler to Fred than it had been to him; at least Pic had hopes of playing football again.

Just one week after Texas had beaten Arkansas 15–14 in a dramatic, nationally televised game on December 6, 1969, Fred Steinmark, who was a junior at Texas and their first-string safety, was told he had a malignant tumor of the left femur (thigh bone). His leg was immediately amputated from the hip. Fred's plight got nationwide publicity, and Brian was perhaps the most empathetic follower of the young ballplayer's medical bulletins.* One afternoon in late January, as Pic stared through the windows at the graceful, snow-covered evergreens that surrounded his home, the words finally came:

* Fred Steinmark died in June 1971.

-64

Dear Fred:

Although I don't know you personally, we have a lot in common. This is why I'm writing you this letter. My football career, just as yours, was brought to a sudden halt this year by cancer, mine in the form of a tumor located directly below my breastbone.

This tumor popped up from nothing to the size of a grapefruit in a period of about three months. I had my surgery on November 28 at Memorial Hospital in New York and missed the last five games of the season.

I watched your game against Arkansas from my hospital bed when I was recovering from surgery and then read about your problem a few days later.

I guess that I, more than any other football player, know how you felt. I spent a lot of time thinking about you and praying for you in those days and that's when I decided I would write. I never got to it until Mike Pyle visited my house when I got home from New York and informed me that you were a Bears fan. He found out through Don (Moon) Mullins of Houston, a former Bear.

Fred, I guess I'd mainly like to share with you my feeling since my operation, simply that our lives are in God's hands, just as they were before our illnesses were known. And I shall never stop praying to God for the strength to carry out the plans He has laid out for me.

I know you are a courageous young man and I hope this letter might be of some help to you. Perhaps some day we may meet one another. I'm sure we would have much to talk about.

Best of luck to you, Fred.

Your friend,
Brian Piccolo

Brian copied the letter over twice. It seemed inadequate. He could only hope that Fred was looking forward to each day as much as he was.

It was going to be hard to leave the children. But after Chicago and New York—after the endless chilly days, Phoenix sounded like heaven. As they boarded the jet, Brian was wondering if he could handle 18 holes of golf for three days, but Beattie had given his enthusiastic approval. "Go ahead," he said, "do anything you feel like doing." It was funny, but Dr. Beattie never acted cautious. He was short on phrases like "bed rest" and "take it easy."

Wigwam Country Club, where the tournament was being held, was in Litchfield Park, Arizona, a few miles out of Phoenix. Some of the hottest athletes in baseball and football made the scene, along with hundreds of spectators and a few dozen of American Airlines' big-paying customers. As if all that glamor wasn't enough, American Airlines grounded a covey of hostesses in Phoenix for the duration. The consensus was that Playboy's bunnies had nothing on AA's stewies.

Brian had been told earlier that his partner was to be Mister Cub, Ernie Banks. He was thrilled. The first thing he did upon arriving was to call Ernie and give him a pep talk.

"I am ready," Ernie told Brian. "Partner, we are going to take it all. Come on over and let's discuss our strategy."

The Chicago Cubs begin training in Scottsdale in February, but Ernie and Eloyce Banks usually bring their three children out to the desert sometime in January. This year Ernie was 39 years old and going into his 18th season of major league baseball.

Joy and Brian found the Bankses lying on the beds in their room watching television and eating potato chips. Joy stretched out on one bed with Eloyce, while Ernie and Brian shared the other. The Bankses and the Piccolos planned how they were going to win the Astro-jet Golf Tournament for Chicago.

The foursome headed by Ernie and Pic finished 15th in a field of 16. The gallery adored them. Brian recognized and greeted every athlete whose path he crossed, and Ernie wondered over his knowledge of baseball—until Brian confided that baseball had been his "real" sport.

"He kept bringing the conversation to me," Ernie said later. "The Cubs had finally come on strong in sixty-seven and sixty-eight after years in the cellar, only to fade in the finish. Brian had a lot of empathy and understanding—and humor—to apply to our situation."

Brian wasn't the world's greatest golfing football player, even when he was well. On the second day Ernie could see that his partner was tiring.

"Let's you and me get back to our wives and get some rest up for tomorrow. It's a sure cinch the other boys'll be out visitin' tonight."

On the morning of the third and final round, Ernie came trundling out in a cart, bending tournament rules. His old knee was bothering him, he told Brian. But after the third hole, he managed to relinquish the cart to the football player. Brian didn't protest. What Ernie didn't know and couldn't have guessed from Brian's enthusiastic participation in the game was a scene that had taken place the night before, when Joy and Brian were alone in their room.

Brian was stretched out on the bed, bare chested. Joy noticed him fingering a part of his body to the left of the sternal scar. Her knees wilted. It was a lump.

"What's that?" she gasped.

What the hell do you think it is? Brian screamed.

Brian and Joy returned from Phoenix on Monday the ninth of February. The trip had been so good, almost like a honeymoon, but landing in Chicago they felt themselves beginning to get uptight again.

Brian stopped by Illinois Masonic Hospital the

next day, taking his new lump in for examination. One of the doctors felt it through his T-shirt. "Don't worry about a thing, Brian," he was told. "It looks like you just pulled a muscle playing golf."

Brian's momentary exultation wore off fast. The cursory examination didn't ring true to him; neither did the flippant diagnosis. He stewed over it for a couple of days.

Finally, on Friday night, Brian picked up the phone and called Dr. Dick Corzatt. His friend was associated with Little Company of Mary Hospital, which was in the neighborhood, so Brian asked Dick where at the hospital he would have to go to get an X ray. He wanted to have a picture taken, he said, to send to Dr. Beattie. Dick was immediately alert. Brian had had X rays at Little Company of Mary before. He knew very well where to go. But Dr. Corzatt replied casually, "Look, I have a scoliosis clinic at the hospital in the morning. Meet me there, and I'll take you up for the X ray."

Brian took the opportunity offered him: he arrived before Dr. Corzatt had finished with the clinic. He took the further opportunity to visit with the youngsters who suffered from the difficult spinal curvature that is scoliosis, and he spoke encouraging words as he related his own battle and victory over cancer. One young man walked out with his father, grinning from ear to ear. He'd forgotten for a time about the full body brace he was wearing.

It didn't take Dr. Corzatt long to make a tentative diagnosis of recurrence when he saw the lemon-sized lump on Brian's pectoral muscle. The primary tumor had been inside the rib cage, and this one was outside, indicating a frightening spread. Dick called in the hospital's chest man to take a look at the X rays with him. Along with the pectoral mass, they saw spots on the left lung.

Dick knew Brian was scared stiff—that was why he had called his friend. Pic needed a friend as much as he needed a doctor. Looking Brian in the eye, saying that, well, maybe it was just a pulled muscle, was the hardest thing Dick Corzatt had ever had to do. Together they called Dr. Beattie in New York. Beattie suggested that Brian fly in for a checkup the next day, Sunday. Brian agreed.

This called for a change of plans. His good friend, Dan Arnold, was expected to fly in on Sunday from dental school in Lincoln, Nebraska, so Brian had to call Dan and tell him their date was off.

Hell, Dan, he said, *I'm sorry but I gotta go back to New York. Another lump.*

Dan shuddered. Brian assured him that it was probably just a broken blood vessel or a pulled muscle—maybe something snapped at the golf tournament.

Finally Dan asked, "Pic, listen, what have you got—and I don't want any of this 'benign neoplasm of the chest' crap—what did the doctor say you had after your operation in November?"

Brian left the phone to get a piece of paper—

he had to be accurate for his semimedical buddy. He returned to read the evil, multisyllable words. Dan copied them.

The next day Dan took his scrap of paper to a pathologist friend. He said, "Listen, if I came in here and told you I had 'malignant mediastinal teratoma, predominantly embryonal cell carcinoma but including sarcoma, seminoma, and squamous carcinoma,' what would you say?"

His friend replied: "I'd say you would be dead within six months."

On February 15th, the phone rang in the 56th
Street apartment of Dorothy and Max Kendrick.

Hi, Dorothy. It was Brian.

"Where are you?" she asked.

*Oh I'm lying in bed over here at the Hilton
East.*

God, no, thought Dorothy. He wasn't due back
until June.

ADMISSION DATE: 2/15/70   PICCOLO, Brian
                                    HOSPITAL #61-54-12
This 26 year old football player was admitted to Memorial Hospital for the 2nd time as an emergency
with swelling in the left pectoral region. He had previously been in Memorial Hospital and on 11/28/69
he had a mediastinal teratoma removed. He was
treated with actinomycin-d for one month with a
plan of being off chemotherapy for two months and
then on again for one month. He had been off chemotherapy for 6 weeks when he noticed the swelling.

PHYSICAL EXAMINATION:
Temperature 98.2; pulse 90; respirations 18; blood pressure 120/70. There is a well healed midline sternal scar, and left anterior chest scar. Just above the incision laterally toward the left axilla, there was a firm, movable, slightly tender, slightly fluctuant mass measuring approximately 6 cm. ....

HOSPITAL COURSE:
On 2/16/70 under local anesthesia, a needle aspiration biopsy was made of the mass. It was "malignant tumor consistent with the previous material." We had consultation with Dr. Golbey of chemotherapy and Dr. D'Angio of radiation therapy. It was felt that an intensive course of chemotherapy was indicated with possibility of surgery later. A skeletal survey, liver scan, and brain scan were negative.

The plan of chemotherapy was: Leukeran 10 mg. daily started on 2/18/70, actinomycin-d 2.5 mg. IV weekly started on 2/19/70, and Methotrexate 5 mg. daily started on 2/20/70. He tolerated this very well. . . .

In spite of their standard outward cheer, the doctors knew that now, with the recurrence, the odds on Brian's survival were short. Dr. Golbey and chemotherapy took command of the attack because long-term control had become the more realistic goal and the drugs were thought to be the best road to that goal. Of course, radiotherapy and surgery were definite recourses for the future.

Brian loathed being sick with the kind of degrading illness caused by chemotherapy. His existence became cyclical; but it wasn't like the football cycle. He'd just be working back into shape and, zap! instead of a game there was another shot. He would take his medicine, sleep, and be ill the next day, and then gradually his strength would build back up. During the high points, Brian would be up and out on the town.

Although they had both agreed that Joy should stay at home with the children during this period, Brian had plenty of company. He enjoyed the warm and generous companionship of Dorothy and Max Kendrick, to whom he had been introduced by Ed McCaskey. Dorothy and Max were confirmed Manhattanites and were well able to show Brian the town. And there was a regular ferry of Pic's friends moving between Chicago and New York. Brian's weight was only off 10 pounds, and on his good days he could eat—and did. Dick Butkus and Ed O'Bradovich from the Bears flew in, and Ron Santo from the Chicago Cubs. Pete Rozelle called often, just to check. Even Brian's favorite legal eagles, Irwin and Sandy, popped in to harass him for a weekend. Irwin remembered that the first thing Brian said when he saw him was, *Hey, let's get out of here. This place is full of sick people.*

And Doc Martin called. He was in New York and wanted to visit, but he caught Brian on a bad day and Pic begged off. Doc could cure a lot of things, considering he wasn't even a doctor. Doc got Brian through college—well, at least through football. He was the head trainer, the 300-pound mother-henning, profane, sublime topkick of the Wake Forest athletic department. Brian loved Doc. Brian loved college. Minoring in academics, Pic sampled just about everything Wake Forest had to offer.

Wake Forest College stands on gently rolling hills in Winston-Salem, North Carolina. In 1956 the school was moved from the town of Wake Forest and built from the ground up with a $21-million grant from the Zachary Smith Reynolds Foundation. Zachary Smith was a relative of R. J. Reynolds and Reynolds tobacco warehouses abound in the area. The college, though, looks like it's been there for a century, so graceful and well-planned are the red-brick Georgian buildings. The campus is dominated by the chapel. But Wake Forest's Baptist beginnings are only slightly felt by the students. The school certainly didn't hesitate to admit one academically average Italian Catholic football player named Brian Piccolo.

Brian didn't tell anyone that Wake Forest and Wichita State were the only colleges in the country to offer him scholarships. He turned down Wichita.

Good thing too, he said later. *That would have put me in Sayers country* [Gale graduated from Kansas U] *and Kansas wasn't big enough for both of us.*

Coach Kurth claims that Brian actually rode into Wake Forest on the tails of his high school teammate, tackle Bill Salter. "They were really interested in the big tackle," Kurth said, "I was able to persuade them that Brian had that something extra that would do the job for them. They were worried about his lack of speed."

Salter did something else for Brian. He fleshed out such a legend that the Salter stories circulating through Wake's athletic culture left Brian with no choice but to be great. "We were all looking around for the future 'stars,' " remembered a fellow frosh recruit, Jim Mayo. "We figured we were in the big-time, and I guess each of us wasn't so sure of himself," said Mayo, "but we knew somewhere there were some *real* big-timers. And here was this bullshit artist, Salter. He had war stories on Brian that were incredible. He'd tell us how the Cubs and Pirates had been panting for Piccolo in baseball; how he was unstoppable on the football field. And the broads! To hear Salter, Brian was like a pasha. Hefner should have it so good. You'd go to check all this out with Brian and he'd say, 'Well . . .' and just smile a lot."

Bill Salter wasn't the only bullslinger at Wake. Brian told a story on his friend Mayo that was still circulating years later. It seems that on one of their traditional spring break trips to the Fort Lauderdale beaches, Brian and Jim were speeding south on Highway 85 when a state policeman stopped them.

The officer said to Mayo, who was driving, "Son, you're speeding."

"I didn't realize that, Sir," Jim replied. "I go to

Wake Forest and I'm trying to get to the beach."

The cop said, "Let me see your driver's license."

"I left in a hurry, Sir, and I don't have my bill-fold," Mayo told him.

"You don't have your billfold? Then let me see your certificate of ownership. It's probably in the glove compartment."

Mayo looked, but it wasn't there.

"Sir," said Jim, "we don't have that either."

"Don't you even know who this car belongs to?" asked the cop. "Don't you know who you are?"

Mayo had a lot of poise. He reached into his pocket and pulled out two dimes. "Sir," he said, "do you know what these are?"

"They're dimes," the officer replied.

"No, Sir," said Mayo. "These are silver bullets and I'm the Lone Ranger."

Mayo swears Brian made the whole thing up.

That first year of football saw Brian star with the Wake Forest Baby Deacons, coached by a former Chicago Bear immortal, Beattie Feathers. The Baby Deacs were 2-3 for the season. Brian scored five touchdowns and four extra points and averaged 4.2 yards per carry. The statistics showed that no yardage was ever lost when Pic had the ball. Ironically, the varsity's first opponent in 1961 was to be Baylor University. Baylor's star fullback that year was future Bear Ronnie Bull, so when the Wake teams gathered on September 28th to begin practice, the freshmen, as fodder for Billy Hildebrand's varsity, were required to run Baylor's offense, and Piccolo became Ronnie Bull, incidentally becoming a fullback. The Baby Deacs were so well trained for that first game that Feathers kept the Baylor offense throughout the season. "I was a helluva Ronnie Bull," said Brian.

Brian Piccolo playing fullback Brian Piccolo gained over 400 yards in his sophomore year, again averaging 4.2 yards per carry.

Our sophomore year we opened up with Army. I have no love for the academies; they kind of destroy your image of the clean-cut American officer—play dirty. I was a little nervous. Although their stadium at West Point holds about thirty-five thousand, this day they had only about two or three thousand out for the game. But they had these microphones sprinkled throughout the cadets in the stands, and when they're turned on it sounds like a hundred thousand fans. And these guys are very rhythmic with their cheers. I was the second-string place-kicker and was out on the field warming up with our first-string place-kicker, when Army took the field and these three thousand or so let out this inhuman cry—I could visualize the Japs coming over the hills in droves, and jezus, next thing I know the center snaps one over my head and hits the place-kicker in the head with another ball. I mean our whole team fell to pieces, and it was just Army taking the field.

Needless to say we didn't go on to conquer the

cadets that day. Or anyone that whole year. We lost all ten games.

If I had known we were going to lose eight more during my junior year before we finally won one—well, it got to where it was really frustrating. You go out to play, and the other teams would keep scoring, and you'd say, "Oh my God, how can we overcome this?" It was just one bad afternoon after another. But finally, and it was homecoming too, we beat South Carolina—Hell, I beat 'em!

I was just so fired up. I had scored a touchdown and I really hamburgered it up. I threw the ball in the stands. After being down nineteen-seven at half time, we were still behind six points, but I was ready. I sensed that we were going to win a game. I carried the ball maybe twenty-two times for a hundred and forty yards or so. Then quarterback and place-kicker Karl Sweetan carried the ball over to tie it nineteen-nineteen. But Karl got hurt in the act of scoring, so I went over to Hildy, and I said, "I'll kick the damn thing!" So I kicked it, and we won twenty-nineteen.

Quarterback Karl Sweetan left Wake after just one year, continuing on a football odyssey that eventually found him with the Los Angeles Rams. That left a spot with the Deacons, which John Mackovic captured.

As a result of the South Carolina victory, Coach Billy Hildebrand was named UPI's college coach of the week, not only for the victory but "for just plain courage under fire." Brian was honorably mentioned by the AP. One local writer commented: "Wake Forest fullback Brian Piccolo will not make the '63 All-Atlantic Coast Conference football team. But when he sits his grandchildren on his knee 30 years from now and shows them his scrapbook, they will be as impressed as if he had made the honor squad."

Brian was extra thrilled to get a letter from Washington Redskin quarterback Norman Snead congratulating him on his performance. Snead, a 1961 graduate of Wake, was his sponsor and a $1,000 contributor to the Deacon athletic scholarship fund. It was good to know at least somebody in the pros was watching you.

You couldn't tell it from his clippings, but Brian wasn't all jock.

When Wake got the Reynolds grant and moved, the fraternities said they would not build individual houses but agreed to sign long-term leases for sections of University-built dormitories. What they had was maybe three rooms downstairs and a straight up section of the dorm. It was very odd. I pledged Sigma Chi when I was a freshman, and it took me about two weeks to realize this was not my bag. Brotherhood's groovy and all of that, but there was just nothing offered. Why should I pay dues just to hang out in one section of the dorm? As a social pledge I could go to everybody's parties—they were always recruit-

ing you. It turned out great, and I could go to all parts of the dorm.

By the time I was a sophomore I had it all mapped out. I took a pretty liberal course but I wanted to go into broadcasting. I majored in speech, minored in business. I was going to really get ready: have a pro football career, go into broadcasting, and with a business minor I'd know how to handle all that money.

You know, when you say you're a speech major, people don't know what all is involved. Hell, I took courses in acting and directing that I tell you were damn tough. In fact, the head of the drama department, Doctor James Walton, persuaded me to stay over the summer after my junior year and play summer stock at Tanglewood Barn Theatre just outside of Winston-Salem. I told him I'd try anything once.

Walton really laid one on me. We did Come Back, Little Sheba, *and I played Turk. If you know the play, Turk is this big dumb athlete who is always on the make for this chick who is an artist. Up until this time Walton had made a fetish of casting a guy in parts that belied his personality. For instance, my first assignment from him, my first scene for crissake, was to play the queer kid lover to the woman of the world in* Tea and Sympathy. *But I worked at it, I really did. Turned out I was a hell of a queer.*

Turk, though, that was typecasting. Opening night was a terror. A bunch of my buddies came out, and wouldn't you know, they sat in the front row. There is this one scene in Sheba *where Turk has to pose as a javelin thrower so the girl can sketch him. So I come out in my shorts and strike this ridiculous stance with a broom for a javelin. I was a little flabby—it was summertime—and I could hear these guys in the front row breaking up. I was trying so hard to stay in character, but I was nervous as hell. I almost cracked.*

I got a good review, though, from the local lady critic. She was an old maid, and I guess just seeing my hairy chest must have done something for her.

Billy Hildebrand was released following Brian's junior football season. In four years as Wake Forest's head coach he had won seven games. One of his players couldn't help describing Hildy: "He was a 'dag nabit,' 'by gum,' southern bible thumpin' gentleman. He was kind and literate and never used profanity. He was the sort of guy you might want your son to play for. You know how they talk about losing games and building character? Hildy was a character builder."

That spring, Wake brought in Bill Tate from the University of Illinois. He had been an assistant under Pete Elliott and had Rose Bowl credentials. As a halfback in 1952 Tate was selected the Most Valuable Player after the Illini's 40-7 defeat of Stanford in the granddaddy of the bowl games. In 1963, he had again journeyed to Pasadena, this time to help direct Dick Butkus, Mike Talliaferro, Jim Grabowski, and Company to victory over Washington. Tate was 32 years old, and Wake was his big chance.

On May 13, 1964, Brian wrote to his buddy Dan Arnold at Florida State in Tallahassee:

Hi Dan,

How the hell are you, stranger? I'm sitting in philosophy class (I don't take all speech courses) right now and I don't feel like taking notes. I figured I'd write this long overdue letter.

I'll recap the issues since I saw you last. Joy and I set the date for December 26, 2:00 p.m. in Atlanta. I want your skinny ass in my wedding and being as you can't be the bride (which isn't a bad thought) I guess you'll have to be an usher. Now goddammit, I won't take no for an answer.

. . . . We got a new coach, coaching staff and athletic director and we are finally going big time. We just finished spring practice and it was tough. I lost 15 pounds in 4 weeks but I look great and picked up a lot of my old scatback speed. I was terrific in the spring game. My team won 40-7 and they held me to 177 yards in 19 carries. That's a little better than 9 yards a carry. That's what I'm going to average next year as I take the National Rushing Championship.

There were some scouts from the Colts and Cowboys there to talk to me. If I have the year I should I don't see how I can keep from making a pretty nice bundle next year. I know I sure could use it being married and all that. Joy will probably get pregnant right away so that money will come in handy. That will be the start of the first million and then you can get your knee pads loose to start crawling to me.

I wish to hell you would occasionally write me a letter. I know being the academic pimp you are you wouldn't write to me during class, so find some time, will you? At least send me a post card so I know you got this letter. Take it easy, lovey.

Always and forever,
Brian

Coach Tate was determined to get off to a good start, so shortly before spring practice he called a meeting at five o'clock one afternoon. This was to be his first session with the players; except for their records he didn't know any of them.

Everyone was on time except Brian, and there was dead silence when Pic walked in five minutes late. "Brian," the new boss barked, "the next time you're late, just don't bother coming." Bill Tate felt that from that moment he had Brian's respect. He never had to tell his star fullback anything more than once.

I remember the first time I met Bill Tate. I was late to a meeting, and he read me out in front of everybody. I was just ready to pop back at him and then I thought, "No, I'd better keep quiet till I see what this guy's got." Turned out he was a winner.

Tate would run a close second to Coach Kurth as "Men Whom I have Respected and Dug a Lot." He came in on a hell of a situation. Out of forty guys or so we had maybe ten who wanted to play, and the rest were willing to ride on their scholarships. There was no question of ability. We were one-nine when I was a junior and five-five when I was a senior with just about the same guys. It was the new coach. He ran off a lot of the trash and got the other guys up off their dead butts and got them going.

Tate was murder on the practice field. He had this real cute system: Two helmets—and if you were a really good boy who gave one hundred percent in practice, you got your helmet painted red and the coach called you a "blue chipper." Only two buys on the team never got one: the quarterback, John Mackovic, and me. Hell, I just can't get enthusiastic about practice. It should be just what it says, practice to prepare yourself for the game. If you hinder your game performance by burning yourself out, that defeats the purpose. Some of the best games I've ever seen have been left on the practice field.

In their Atlantic Coast Conference opener in 1964, Wake Forest beat Virginia, 31-21. The star of the game was 168-pound quarterback, John

Mackovic. He accounted for 267 yards rushing and passing, using the bootleg for most of his 131 yards on the ground. Mackovic scored one touchdown and Piccolo scored the other three. Somebody else kicked the field goal.

On the way home from the game, Coach Tate sat through what he felt was an uplifting experience. "Here we were on the bus, a bunch of college boys and a few coaches and this guy Piccolo who, for the moment at least, was the super star, and his buddy, Jim Mayo, get up in front of the bus and lead the entire team in a four-hour community sing. It was a clean sing too—your grandmother would have loved it. Coming from the Big Ten the previous year, I'll tell you it was refreshing. Up there we never relaxed. Not even after victories."

Bill Tate had been so impressed with Washington's option offense in the Rose Bowl—even though his own boys beat it—that he adopted it as his own and brought it south with him. "Coaches are notorious thieves," Tate confessed.

The option offense was dependent upon the inside fake to the fullback coming either off tackle or breaking back against the flow. Tate designed the system so that the quarterback was either going to give the ball to Pic, or fake it to Pic and stay to the outside with a quarterback keeper, or pitch to a trailing halfback. Consequently, with the threat of Brian coming up inside all the time, the linebackers were kept honest. If they watched for Brian, the Deacons went outside with the option—

which was precisely what had happened in the opening game. But later in the season, when teams began to compensate to the outside, Brian killed them off tackle.

"Brian had exceptional balance at the line of scrimmage, the ability to maneuver in a small area and a great feel inside. When the linebackers started flowing, he could break back against the tide. Brian would kill the teams that flowed too fast to stop our outside offense. This was the entire concept."

Tate was lucky. He didn't know going in that he had the fullback necessary to make his system work. Piccolo made it work. The year following Brian's graduation Tate wasn't so fortunate.

But meanwhile, in the '64 season, Wake was picked by all the experts to finish dead last in the ACC. They had the weakest record, and with 48 members, the smallest squad in the conference. But they had a new coach with fresh ideas, a talented albeit unseeded quarterback in John Mackovic; and they had Piccolo, with his toughness, his all-encompassing spirit, and his hunger. Above all, his hunger to win. Wake ended the season at 5-5; but to read the local press or talk to any of the men involved, an observer would swear the Deacons had gone to the Rose Bowl.

The first game of the season had set the spirit. After scoring three touchdowns against the Virginia Cavaliers, Piccolo galloped joyously down the field with Mackovic carrying the ball on his bootleg that turned into an 87-yard scoring scamper. For the last 20 yards Pic was yelling to Mack for the lateral. The quarterback was about to break Brian's record as the only member of the Wake varsity who had ever scored a touchdown!

In their second game Wake demolished Virginia Tech, and the AP reported, "Ray Handly of Stanford leads the nation in rushing with 252 yards on 35 carries, five yards ahead of Brian Piccolo of Wake Forest. Piccolo, Joe Namath of Alabama, and a Syracuse sophomore, Floyd Little, share the scoring lead with 30 points each."

The Deacons lost the third game to North Carolina. Another fullback starred in that one, Ken Willard of the Tar Heels. They went under again the following week, losing to Vanderbilt. The fifth game of the year was to be played at home in Bowman Gray Stadium against Clemson. It was homecoming, and Joy was coming in from Atlanta for the weekend.

Brian and Joy hadn't seen each other since the previous summer when they had become formally engaged. The act of engagement itself was a typical Piccolo event, at once profound and irreverent.

The day was hot, and Joy had taken Carol out in the backyard of her parents' Atlanta home to cool off in a shallow wading pool. There was an enduring love between the sisters. Joy did not resent the extra responsibility that Carol's condition had forced on her as she grew up.

Brian sneaked in the front door unseen by the girls. When he spied them outside he quickly changed into his trunks. With a great flourish he

dashed out the back door and leaped into the pool
—and most of the water leaped out. Embracing
both Joy and Carol, Brian said, *I have something
for my two best girls.* Then he slipped a beautiful
diamond solitaire on Joy's finger and gave a smaller
—but somehow just as beautiful—ring to Carol. Joy
Murrath and Brian Piccolo were betrothed. "But
the only one he kissed was Carol!" Joy said.

Brian could have used some extra kisses himself over homecoming weekend. Wake lost to
Clemson 21-2. Still, John Mackovic picked up 242
yards to continue to lead the conference in total
offense, and Piccolo continued to romp ahead of
the pace toward the ACC rushing record of 1,010
set in 1956 by Wake back Bill Barnes. And Pic was
still second in national rushing.

One of Piccolo's practice ploys, part of his determination never to slip up and earn the blue
chipper's red helmet, was his fairly constant complaint of minor injuries during the week. Actually
Brian went through his entire football career without a disabling injury, but at Wake Forest he dear-
ly loved having his trainer, big Doc Martin, cluck-
ing over him—or swearing at him—as the case might
be. That was Doc's philosophy: Gentle care and
give 'em hell. Treat the injury and deny it exists.
It was just what Brian craved.

Lewis Martin (Brian called him Luigi but everybody else called him Doc) was a big man. His small
brown eyes were buried in a beefy face, and they
would glint and smile with equal impact. Doc was
a legend in the Wake Forest athletic department.

Stories of his secret kindnesses abound, like the time he laid out the money so scholarship student and quarterback Norman Snead could buy a wedding ring and a suit to get married in, although marriage is not one of bachelor Martin's favorite institutions. Or another time, when one of his players contracted leukemia and Doc moved in and quietly nursed the boy for eight months. Doc filled a need for Brian, just as the head coach did.

It's pretty much an old story to hear an athlete say that had he not been in sports he might have ended up on the street. Sometimes it's true. But simply occupying a boy's otherwise idle time is not the key; it's also the discipline, the physical care, and the strong male image projected by many coaches. The team is a substitute family for many athletes. It was for Brian. And he would do anything to gain its attention, its approval, and its love.

Brian felt very strongly about the importance of the trainer to an athletic team.

You have your team well conditioned, and you give them a top-notch trainer with the best equipment, and you're a step ahead in the win column.

Wake hadn't suffered any injuries going into the sixth game of the '64 season against Maryland in College Park. But they'd suffered three defeats. Piccolo wasn't hungry, he was starving. The Deacons were listed as 14-point underdogs.

Methodical Mackovic hung in all the way against the Maryland Terrapins, passing brilliantly to Joe Carazo and Dick Cameron. With 1:50 remaining on the clock, the Deacons were down 17-14, but they were on the Terps 15-yard line with a first down, with only one way to go. On his third successive plunge, with 166-pound halfback Joe Carazo making the key block, Piccolo scored. Then he kicked the extra point and Wake Forest won, 21-17. Pic gained 110 yards on 27 carries that afternoon. On October 27, 1964, the AP out of New York announced that Brian Piccolo was leading the nation in rushing by 63 yards.

At this point, Bill Tate, who was given neither to singling out players nor to effusive compliments, told Mary Garber of the *Winston-Salem Twin City Sentinel*, "I don't think there is a player in America who has meant as much to his team. Every defense is set for him. If Pic gets his 1,000 yards for the season I don't see how they (the All America selectors) can ignore him. And they sure can't ignore him as the Number 1 rusher in the nation. Statistics are important."

Years later, Brian, always his own best PR man, would tell Chicago sportswriters, his coaches, or anybody else who might be able to help him get into a game: *I won't get eighty yards in one play, but I'll get them for you in eight.* Nobody listened.

Of all the bouncing balls, the football is the most unpredictable—which is what excites the customers. But it's not one of the joys of the trade as far as the participants are concerned. Here was Wake Forest, with the nation's leading rusher and the league's leading passer, beating the good teams and losing to the bad ones. Lady Luck was fickle as hell. The Deacons had beaten Memphis State in the eighth game of the season in every statistical category—except the score, which was 23-14 in favor of Memphis. The coach had said statistics are important. But some are importanter than others.

It was inevitable that the newspapers would begin to do things with the name "Piccolo." Athletes tend to become elaborately unconcerned about the press. But Brian never pretended to be indifferent to publicity. He loved it. "Piccolo Plays Winning Tune," said one paper. "The Sweetest Music this Side of Heaven Comes from a Piccolo," bannered another. One columnist led off with a beaut: "Little Piccolo puts out like 76 trombones." A particularly nifty quote, this one from Duke coach Bill Murray, really got to Brian. Murray told his boys, "This year we're going to play taps on Piccolo."

Bowman Gray Stadium, Wake Forest's home field, was not the garden spot of Winston-Salem, North Carolina. It was across town from the campus and was used regularly not only by Wake but also by Winston-Salem State and four city high school football teams. Bowman Gray has since been replaced by Groves Stadium, located on campus. By November 7th, when Duke came to town, the field was in a notably rotten condition. Brian had never seen Bowman Gray when, as a prospective recruit, he had been flown in for the red carpet rush. The stadium was always left off the guided tour.

Wake hadn't beaten Duke since 1951. The

Deacons were due, and the Blue Devils just happened to walk into the wrong place at the right time. It was 93 degrees and very dusty at Bowman Gray that afternoon. In that setting, as one student reporter put it, "The Baptists smote the Methodists 20-7." Piccolo gained 115 yards and lost 15 pounds. He caught three passes and carried the ball 36 times to smash the ACC record. Brian had had to fight for every inch because not only was Duke out to protect its conference lead, but the Blue Devils were still looking for a bowl bid. By hand, on foot, and by toe, Piccolo scored all 20 points. After the game a Duke assistant told the press: "We worked all week on stopping three things: Piccolo's running, the quarterback pass to the fullback, and the option play. Wake did exactly what we expected them to do and they beat hell out of us doing it."

All year Brian had been highly successful in moving the first-down marker on third-down plays, but in the game against Duke, he achieved near perfection—making it seven times out of eight attempts. This was one of the most significant points about his performance and a stat to impress the professionals, but Brian claimed that the only thing the pros noticed about the victory was his postgame weight: he was down to 185 pounds.

Duke's defeat gave the Deacons an outside chance to share the conference title; and both the UPI and *Sports Illustrated* named Piccolo the Back of the Week.

On Saturday the Deacs went to Columbia. Brian

scored all Wake's points, but South Carolina won, 23-13. The next week the word out of New York was: "The big questions left unanswered in the major college football statistics issued Tuesday are whether Howard Twilley of Tulsa can outscore Brian Piccolo of Wake Forest, whether David Ray of Alabama will top the field-goal record, and whether Southern Cal's Mike Garrett can threaten Piccolo's hold on the rushing lead."

The final game of Brian's college career was to be played against North Carolina State. The State Wolfpack had only to beat or tie Wake to take the Atlantic Coast Conference championship. It was a heady year for Wake. The Deacons gaveth and the Deacons tooketh away. In this case, they took the title away from State and gave it back to Duke. The Deacons beat the Wolfpack 27-13. They had come full circle, and as in the first game of the season, Piccolo scored three touchdowns and John Mackovic the fourth.

Brian ended the season with both the Atlantic Coast Conference and the National rushing and scoring titles, with 1,044 yards and 111 total points. Nationally, he nosed out Jim Grabowski of Illinois in rushing, and Howard Twilley, a receiver whose quarterback was Jerry Rhome of Tulsa, in scoring. When someone asked Brian if he was aware of the record situation on the field during the final game, he was typically candid.

Sure I knew I was close to the record. Sure I knew when I broke it. I heard the guy on the public address system. I always do.

Brian summed up the season and the whole Deacon perspective for sportswriters as he lay, weak and happy, on the bench after carrying the ball 34 times against North Carolina State.

We beat Duke, he panted, *and we beat State. They are the two top teams in the conference standings. The way I figure it, that makes us about Number One.*

Nearby, Coach Bill Tate was telling the press, "I think we have made history by finishing third." The Rose Bowl should have been so glorious.

Now it was time for the payoff. The pro draft was coming up the next Saturday. The all-star game selectors were lining up their teams, and the All America lists were being compiled. Brian Piccolo was the Atlantic Coast Conference's Most Valuable Player—a sure thing All American.

I started out close to the top in both rushing and scoring, and I just stayed up there all year. I was lucky—and I had a good coach, a canny trainer, and some very decent blocking. It was a tremendous thrill. You just never think something like that's going to happen. But everything fell into place, and when it was over I came out on top.

At about the middle of the season I'd started hearing from sportswriters from all over the country—something that had never happened to me before. I felt fantastic. I was looking ahead. When I gave up baseball I had decided on professional football. I never considered anything else from the time I entered Wake. You might think that sounds ridiculous; but I figure you got to decide what you're going to do, then how you're going to do it, and then do it.

During the course of the year I had been getting letters from the pro teams. I found out later that they were just form letters—that hundreds and hundreds of guys get them. Even before my good senior year I figured that with my usual performance I'd get a shot somewhere in pro ball, but after having had the season I had, I thought I'd go pretty high in the draft.

Then, when I was assigned an NFL baby-sitter, I thought jezus, I'm gonna be a number-one pick! The draft was held on the Saturday of our Thanksgiving vacation in nineteen sixty-four. Now it's held in January, which I think is a lot better for the college boys.

On Monday I'd received a call from this guy who wanted to know where I was planning to spend my holidays. I explained to him that I was getting married December twenty-sixth in Atlanta, but was scheduled for the North-South Shrine game in Miami on the twenty-fifth, so I wouldn't be in town the week before my wedding, and I had to go down to Atlanta over Thanksgiving to take care of those few things that the groom has to do, you know, like buy a ring and get fitted for a tux.

Well, this guy wanted to take me to the Bahamas, for crissake! A bunch of my buddies or my fiancee or whomever I wanted could come along. The guy's name was Tony Smilgin, and he worked

In Fort Lauderdale, his home town, Brian made an early start in football—every local all-star team. Pictured with him are brothers Joe (52) and Don (4).

Brian made backfield when a senior in high school and was unmatched at telling locker-room war stories. Holding the ball for his practice kick is his friend Dan Arnold.

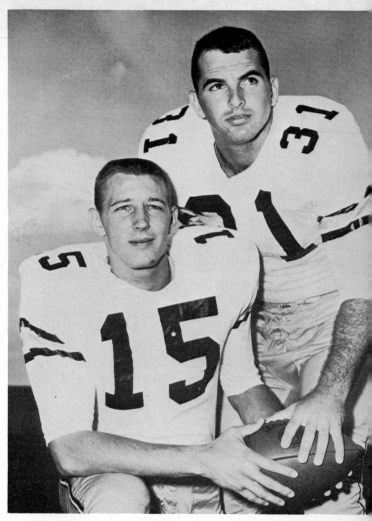

Brian majored in speech at Wake Forest. He and John Mackovic, QB, were the star combination that brought the Deacons a "winning" season. Brian held both the ACC and National titles in rushing (1,044 yards) and scoring (111).

Brian's rookie year with the Bear organization was 1965. Standing behind him and Gale Sayers, his friend and roommate, while they were taking a breather during an exhibition game with the Cleveland Browns, is linebacker Bill George (61), now retired. ▶

In his short season as a Bear, Brian made 5 Tds (the one here at Wrigley Field), gained 927 yards rushing and 537 yards in pass-receiving.

(Opposite) When a sports photographer would order a typical "Look tough!" shot, Brian cast himself in the role—he'd typically respond by clenching a fist and then go into method ham acting.

LORI   KRISTI   BRIAN   JOY   TRACI

for the state of Florida. Baby-sitting was just a part-time job with him. He was an NFL man, and this was when the leagues were at war, before the common draft. Smilgin's job was to take me and hide me from the American League.

I told Smilgin where I'd be, and he turned up in Atlanta with a big suite of rooms rented for me at the Holiday Inn. He called me at Joy's just before the draft was to start and said, "Come on down." So I went—nothing to lose. First thing he told me was, "Anything you want, you name it, you got it, just sign the tab and have a good time."

Now, I've never been accused of being too bright, but I'm smart enough to know that people just don't offer things like that without a catch. So I said, "What's the pitch?" And he explained that he was to sign me as soon as I was picked and before I got a chance to talk to the American League. It turned out I had the greatest baby-sitter in the history of baby-sitting, because not only did the American League not draft me, but the National League didn't draft me either. They had completely forgotten where I was.

You know it was funny—well, not really funny. I felt uncomfortable for my baby-sitter too. We sat together through the first round. There were only fourteen teams, but the first round took something like sixteen hours. And when you're thinking all the time that the next one might be you, that's a helluva long time. Ken Willard went right off the top to San Francisco. Mike Curtis went in the first round too—both of them backs in my con-

ference. I wasn't too disappointed, though, about the first round. "What the hell," I told Smilgin, "two or three isn't bad with the money those guys are paying."

Then they went through the second round and the third round, and when they got up to around seven and eight, I began to wonder what was going on. During the course of this thing I'd gone out for a walk, moved around; hell, it was driving me crazy. Finally, when it was over and I didn't get picked—well, I could hardly believe it. Four hundred and forty draftees and none of 'em me. I was disappointed and embarrassed. Really embarrassed.

And I couldn't understand it. I kept thinking there must have been a mistake. The feeling I had, I guess, was the closest thing to the feeling I got when they told me about the tumor. It was something that shouldn't have happened, but it did. It wasn't so much because I wanted my name up in lights, but because I had worked and waited so long to know where I was going to be playing professional football, and here I was—bypassed— and I still didn't know.

But what the hell, it didn't take me long to bounce back. I was bound and determined then— not to show the league—but to prove to myself that I could play. What did I care about them? I figured they couldn't be very smart if they didn't draft me.

Around this time too the All America teams began to come out. I made most of them. But in the two "important" ones, the AP and UPI, I was second string. The wonderful Associated Press had me on second-string defense. I was in for two defensive plays all year. On one I kept a Virginia touchdown drive going because I got a fifteen-yard penalty. This guy was running out for a pass, and the ball was thrown on the ground in front of him. But the whistle hadn't blown, and as long as I was out there I thought I might as well hit him. On the other play, against Duke, I made the tackle. I realize it was a hell of a tackle—but jezus, I didn't hit him that good!

It just goes to show you, an honest man can't really be too honored or thrilled by these things. There's so much bull in college PR. And don't kid yourself—public relations guys really influence the voting. You find that out at these all-star games, when you actually play with and against the guys that you've read about during your entire college career. You go there with something concrete in your mind about what these guys are going to be like, and you know, I don't think I was right on any of them. Some are much better than you expected and some are nothing. You figure, my God, what a hoax!

In the North-South game I was, for instance, impressed with Jack Snow. I thought then and still think he's an underrated receiver. And Bob Hayes—I mean I knew he was the world's fastest human and all, but I didn't figure he could play football—but he could. One guy I wasn't impressed with—personality-wise—was the Kansas Comet,

Gale Sayers. What an arrogant son of a bitch. I didn't see him speak to a soul the whole week we were together.

Going into that game in Miami on December twenty-fifth, I was still a free agent. Baltimore, Chicago, and Cleveland had all contacted me, and I felt their interest was genuine. I figured if I had a good game it wouldn't hurt me at all. Also, I finally thought I was going to get my proof, after all those years, that I was better than Tucker right there at home in the Orange Bowl in Miami. I actually started at fullback and Frederickson was on the bench. I picked up some yards, made a couple of first downs, nothing sensational. I'll tell you one thing: Knowing the pros were watching, I started blocking to beat hell. But every time we got into scoring position that damn coach—I won't mention his name—would take out me and Larry Dupree of Florida and put in Frederickson and Ken Willard, the "big backs," to carry the ball over. Every time. I couldn't believe it.

They couldn't believe it in Atlanta either.

Some 30 or so of Joy's and Brian's relatives were gathered in her parents' home on Christmas afternoon to feast and watch the bridegroom play football. The Murraths had prepared a huge luncheon buffet and placed television sets throughout the house so no one would miss a play. It was a hilarious day, and everyone enjoyed it; well, almost everyone. Irene Piccolo had renewed a grudge against the man she considered her son's old cross-town rival, Tucker Frederickson, and spent the afternoon cursing the bad judgment of the South's head coach, Wayne Hardin, for never allowing her son to score.

The future Mrs. Brian Piccolo wasn't very happy either. Joy was depressed. "Depressed?" said Brian's boyhood pal, Dan Arnold, who arrived in the midst of the fun and confusion. "She wasn't depressed. Joy was madder than hell."

Joy and Brian had originally scheduled the wedding on the day after Christmas, thinking that there would be no way in which any football activities could interfere on the 26th of December. And then the Shrine game came up. Whoever heard of a football game on Christmas Day? With all the relatives in from Syracuse and other distant places, activities had to be planned to the minute. And the wedding rehearsal was to be at 9:00 P.M. on Christmas night. That's why Dan had come in; he had agreed to be an usher. Everyone, in fact, was there except Brian. But Brian had promised Joy he would catch the six o'clock plane out of Miami and would be there on time—even if he had to leave before the game ended. Joy swore he had promised.

The game didn't start until three o'clock in the afternoon—another piece of bad luck. The television announcer was somehow aware of Piccolo's dilemma, and he kept the nationwide audience—and Joy—apprised of the probabilities of Brian Piccolo's making it to his rehearsal or—for that matter—to the wedding the next day!

Every time Brian came trotting off the field, Joy would watch to see if he continued on into the locker room. She was glued to the television set, and she took a lot of good-natured ribbing from her relatives, who thought she was naïve to expect Brian to leave a football game for anything.

She should have known better. He never even looked at the clock.

The game ended shortly after Brian's intended flight left Miami for Atlanta. In the meantime, 60 friends and relatives had joined the wedding party, including the subdued bride, for dinner at Mammy's Shanty, and had then gone on to the rehearsal at Immaculate Heart of Mary Church. Sometime during the course of the evening, Brian's oldest brother, Joe, who was best man, received a telegram from the wayward groom: Brian would arrive on the 4:00 A.M. plane.

Joe picked up Brian at the airport and let him get a couple of hours' sleep at a local motel before dragging him over to Joy's home on the morning of the wedding. Joe knew it was bad form for the groom to see the bride before the ceremony on their wedding day, but he also knew that Joy wouldn't believe Brian was in town unless she saw him.

Brian blew through the kitchen door, flung his arms wide, and declared,

I'm here bride, I'm ready.

Joy glared at him, her wide hazel eyes filling with tears.

"Brian," she wailed, "the rehearsal! You promised."

A grin slowly enveloped his face as he crossed the room. *Hell, Joy,* he said, *you know I hate practice.*

She fell into his arms.

The Nuptial Mass that afternoon was a glorious affair, which included a papal blessing. Monsignor Michael J. Regan officiated; he also sang "Ave Maria," which everyone agreed was especially effective. The reception following the ceremony was held in the grand ballroom of the Americana Hotel and was gay, with music and dancing and a sumptuous sit-down dinner for 250 guests. Brian loved it. He reveled in his wedding's old country richness.

Thank you, Mamma, he told Grace at one point, *it couldn't have been better.*

Toward seven o'clock in the evening, the bride and groom prepared to cut the wedding cake. Brian gave the traditional first taste to Joy, and then, as the guests watched quietly, he carried another bit of his wedding cake down to the end of the table where Carol was slumped in her wheelchair. He bent and kissed his crippled little sister-in-law as he fed her the tiny piece of cake.

I love you, he said.

There was one bit of decoration at the party that had to be explained over and over again. In the middle of the buffet, cooling the shrimp, was a huge bear carved in ice. It seemed that Brian had received a call from George S. Halas. The Old Man had offered the Piccolos a honeymoon, should they choose to spend it in Chicago. It looked like Brian Piccolo was going to be a Chicago Bear.

By March 10th, Brian had been on chemotherapy for almost a month. He'd had it with the hospital. He'd had it with chemotherapy. He'd had it with New York. Brian wanted to go home. His blood count was low enough. The time had come to stop the course of drugs. Chemotherapeutic agents attack the most rapidly dividing cells of the body which, in addition to those of the blood-producing bone marrow, in Brian included those of the tumor. If the blood count was low, then blood cell production had been arrested and, it was hoped, so had the production of tumor cells.

The drugs had not been successful to the point of eliminating the need for surgery, however; Brian would have his left pectoral muscle, his entire left breast, removed in two weeks. A mastectomy, they called it. But he was in no shape for surgery now.

Twenty minutes after Dr. Beattie told him he could return to Chicago for a rest, Brian was on his way to LaGuardia. He was going to be home for Traci's birthday after all.

One thing Brian could not bear to talk about during his prolonged visits to Memorial were his children.

It hurts me even to think about the girls, he said once in a rare moment, revealing his inner agony.

But being with Lori, Traci, and Kristi was something else again. To Brian, there was nobody more fun than a little kid—especially if it was his own little kid.

Joe and Ann Smith lived next door to the Piccolos during their early years in the little house in Beverly Hills. Ann remembers that it was a daily ritual to look from her kitchen window into the Piccolos' and watch Brian singing and dancing his tiny daughters around the room as Joy was preparing their dinner. And almost any day when Brian was home, a neighborhood youngster could knock on the door, ask Joy if Brian could play, and that's all it would take: Pic would be out in the front yard playing ball with the little boys. He was a born Pied Piper. Joy had many quiet hours in the summertime, simply because her husband was happy to spend an afternoon splashing in the backyard wading pool with Lori and Traci. And when Kristi was born on Christmas Day of 1968, Brian was on the telephone for hours announcing to all his friends:

I have another little princess.

Small wonder then that Brian tended to make a Hollywood production out of birthday parties. There had to be at least two dozen balloons, all blown up, and tied everywhere around the room. Joy's responsibility ended when the actual party began. Brian ran the whole show—the distribution of cake and ice cream, the games, the opening of presents. The Piccolos had invited the Kureks, the Sayers, and the Concannons from the Bears, and several other close friends and their children for Traci's all-day affair on March 16th.

The Chicago Bulls, who sometimes honored players outside of the basketball ranks, had given Brian a "Night" in February, and one of his gifts had been a pool table. It was delivered on the day before the party, and after dinner the men inaugurated it. All his life Brian had wanted a big rec room with a pool table. His was used for the first and last time at Traci's party.

Pic wisecracked and sweet-talked his way throughout the day. But sometimes, in the quiet moments, his guests caught a faraway look in Brian's deep brown eyes. Traci Piccolo had an unforgettable third birthday party; her daddy saw to that.

Brian's respite was brief. On the 22nd the Piccolos went back to New York. On the 24th Dr. Beattie performed the mastectomy.

ADMISSION DATE: 3/22/70   PICCOLO, Brian
                                 HOSPITAL #61-54-12
This professional football player had a malignant teratoma removed at Memorial Hospital on November 28, 1969 through a sternal splitting and left anterior chest incision. There was one lymph-node posi-

tive in the superior mediastinum which contained embryonal cell carcinoma. Additionally, areas of sarcoma, seminoma, squamous carcinoma, and choriocarcinoma were seen in the tumor. He convalesced uneventfully, and actinomycin-d, which had been started preoperatively, was to be continued. He was admitted to Memorial Hospital for the second time on February 15, 1970 with a mass in his left pectoral muscle and densities in his left lung field. A decision was made to start him on intensive quadruple chemotherapy on 2/18/70. He received a combination of Leukeran, Vincristine, actinomycin-d, and Methotrexate. Again the plan was to continue this until 3/10/70 and then interrupt the chemotherapy for two weeks. He was to be readmitted to reevaluation.

PHYSICAL EXAMINATION:
The patient appeared relatively well. His temperature was 100°; pulse 100; respirations 24; blood pressure 104/70; weight 194 lbs. There were no palpable cervical or axillary lymph-nodes. The incisions were well healed. There was a tense, slightly tender, fluctuant mass in his left pectoral muscle measuring 10 cm. in diameter. The rest of the examination was within normal limits.

ADMISSION LABORATORY DATA:
... A chest X ray showed a clear right lung, but there were areas of increased density scattered through the left lung, mostly in the lower lung field. A skeletal survey was negative. A liver scan on 4/1/70 likewise was negative.

It was felt that these lesions had not responded well to chemotherapy. Since no other lesions had appeared and the lesion in the pectoral muscle was getting larger and uncomfortable, a radical mastectomy and axillary lymphnode dissection should be carried out. . . .

Brian and Joy shared a dream, and once in a while, during the long days of recuperation in the hospital, they talked about it: Someday when the girls were older and Brian just had one job instead of the several he was tied into as a professional football player, they were going to go on a long romantic trip—just the two of them—because neither had ever had the chance to travel. For damn sure, they promised themselves, they'd find a way to bypass New York.

There had been one romantic trip for the Piccolos already, a honeymoon to Chicago, only five years before. It seemed more like 5o.

Coach Bill Tate had strongly recommended his star fullback to the Bears, but when he heard over the Christmas holidays that Brian might indeed be signing with Chicago, he called from Winston-Salem with a last bit of caution. "I'll never forget my one season with the Bears, Brian," he said. "A fellow rookie, a friend of mine, fumbled a couple of times in an exhibition game. You really had to feel sorry for the guy. After the second fumble Halas took him out, and as the youngster came to the sidelines the Old Man put a fatherly arm around his shoulders. The crowd was sympathetic to the rookie's plight and seeing this show of affection, broke into applause. But Halas was telling the kid. 'Listen, you son of a bitch, you do that again and your ass is gone from here.'"

Brian got the message. He knew it wasn't going to be easy; but unlike many of his peers, he was not in awe of George Halas. Actually, he couldn't wait to meet him. Anybody who at age 70 was still coaching football and, not only that, was running the whole Chicago Bear business enterprise, had to be a helluva man. The only thing that bothered Pic was the rumor that Halas threw nickels around like they were manhole covers.

Brian and Joy hadn't been in Chicago more than a few hours when the word went out that the Bears were calling a press conference on December 29th. Such a notification would cause a bare nod of the head from sportswriters who cover big league sports in most cities of the nation; teams call press conferences all the time—it gets them attention, and it's good public relations. But the Bears don't particularly like to draw attention to themselves, and they don't need devices to do so anyhow. The Bears are a Chicago institution, and even nonfootball fans keep abreast of their affairs. The reason is George Halas himself. He is a part of Chicago, one of those adored, bedeviled, arbitrary, stubborn, and powerful men who make up the Establishment and account for a good part of the image of "The city of the big shoulders."

"Son of a gun," they were saying in newsrooms all over town, "the Old Man's gone and called a press conference. Do you suppose he's retiring?"

The possibility of Halas's retirement had been the speculation preceding every press conference announced in the past 25 years.

Cooper Rollow of the *Chicago Tribune* said it best after the mystery had been explained:

> "Coach George Halas of the Chicago Bears called a press conference yesterday noon in the swank Mid America Club on the 39th floor of the Prudential building.
>
> "Was it to announce the appointment of George Wilson, ex-Detroit Lions coach to the coaching staff? Was it to announce that linebacker Bill George had been elevated from player to coaching status? Was Halas himself quitting?
>
> "No to all three rumors.
>
> "It was to reveal the signing of Brian Piccolo.
>
> "Brian Piccolo?"

Up and down, Brian's fortune had gone—all his life. But now he was riding high.

I fell in love with Chicago right away—"My kind of town," as the song goes. But that wasn't the most important reason I signed. You're going to find this hard to believe, but the Old Man offered me the most money. That's right. I was talking to Cleveland and Baltimore too, but Chicago offered me the most—which doesn't say a lot for my contract. Papa Bear doesn't have a reputation for being a big spender.

And there was another reason the Bears looked good to me: They had the lowest team average in rushing the year before, nineteen sixty-four. I figured they needed help. Fortunately for Bear fans, and unfortunately for me, they got it—from Gale Sayers. But right then I wasn't worried about Sayers. There are a lot of first-round draft choices who can't cut it in the pros. I don't care what BLESTO V (the Bears' scouting combine) says. There's more to it than the almighty computer and how fast a guy can run the forty.

The press party they threw for Joy and me was really something. I don't know what made the Old Man do it; so far as I know he hasn't done it since. Naturally, the big question from all the writers was why hadn't I been drafted. To this day I don't know, but I entertained 'em with the two ridiculous stories I had gotten.

It seemed that a guy from a school similar to Wake Forest—if you can imagine that—with a name similar to mine—if you can imagine the two of them together—had been drafted in the early rounds, and they thought I was already gone.

The explanation that is probably true—though no excuse—is that the story got around that I was five-ten and a hundred eighty-five pounds. Those great scouting systems! Why didn't somebody come down and put me on a scale? Why didn't they measure me?

I met a lot of poeple at that press conference who would later become friends. But my favorite that day was CBS sportscaster Bruce Roberts. He came up to me with his notebook and pencil in hand and said, "Okay, Brian, how tall would you like to be, how much do you plan to weigh, and how fast would you like me to say you can run the forty?"

That Roberts was a helluva reporter.

I was selected to play in the Coach's All America game in June. Actually, I didn't play in the game—I pulled a hamstring in practice. It was a mistake to participate in the first place. I don't blame the guys you read about who don't want to play in those all-star games—you know, the big stars who have a chance to make good money in the pros. I'd never do it again.

Anyhow, when I got to my rookie training camp in July, my leg still wasn't right. And I was really worried.

But evaluating the personnel at this time, I thought I definitely had a good chance to make the team. I just wished that my leg would heal so that I could. I really didn't feel a part of things, you know, not being able to practice. It's funny, pro ballplayers understand when a guy's hurt, because I came to be the same way when I later saw rookies who were hurt for a long time. But with a pulled hamstring you can go to practice every day because you're not physically in bad shape, you just can't run. I got to a point where I felt like I might have been resented by a lot of guys. Here I was, just standing around. I started thinking that the veterans were probably saying, "Why the hell don't they get rid of him, get him out of here?"

But I hung in there, and I figured I'd stick because they were down to forty-two players when they put me on waivers. In a peculiar way the injury worked to my advantage. I hadn't played in any exhibition games, so no one had seen what I could do, and of course, the word was out about my hamstring. So I cleared waivers, and they offered me a job on the taxi squad.

A lot of the guys you see now on pro football teams have spent time on the taxi squad. Believe me, it's no fun. You practice with the team, but you don't really belong. You don't suit up on Sundays. With the Bears we had separate but unequal locker areas. And then, sixty-five was one of those years when nobody got hurt. Mind you, you don't want to see a guy hurt, but that's your ticket off the cab squad.

And my rookie season—that was the one year I really busted my tail in practice.

The Bears had another Wake Forest graduate, and his name was Bill George. Bill had for years been the number-one name in pro football defense and was credited along with former Bear defensive coach Clark Shaughnessy with developing the position of middle linebacker. Ironically, Bill himself ended up on the taxi squad in 1965.

If Brian had feelings of insecurity, he didn't show them during that first training camp. Bill George took the rookie under his wing, and Pic spent most of his social hours listening to the incomparable tall tales of glory and gore that offensive lineman Stan Jones, fullback Joe Marconi, defensive end Doug Atkins, Bill George, and the other old vets loved to spin. A few years later, Brian and Ralph Kurek would try to revive this custom. "How can we have a future without a past?" Ralph would ask. But both Brian and Ralph felt that the younger ballplayers were becoming less interested. Pro football was changing.

During the practice week, the job of the seven men allotted by league rule to the taxi squad, augmented by some of the lower-ranking rostered players, was to run the Sunday opponents' offense or defense, as the case might be, so the Bears' opposite number could practice against the formations and plays they expected to see in the upcoming game. Brian figured that since he was locked into the junior offense, he'd damn well better enjoy it. So he created his own team with its own name, the Beavers, and with its own special kind of pride, not to mention its own "special" locker room and tattered towels.

The Beavers played their hearts out. Brian captained the Beaver offense, and Bill George captained the Beaver defense. Ralph was low man on the backfield roster, so he ran at fullback while Brian ran at halfback. Larry Rakestraw was the quarterback. Rakestraw and Piccolo would combine on what they called the Beaver pass of the week. It was especially satisfying when the Beavers were playing the roles of the Green Bay Packers. Brian was Paul Hornung and Larry was Bart Starr. One of the Pack's favorite plays was termed a "66 star pass" by the Bears. On a two-second delay that would bring in the Bear linebackers, Piccolo/Hornung would swing out through the split end and wide receiver, sprinting straight down the field to catch Rakestraw/Starr's pass on about the five and crash into the end zone for the score. It was always sensational.

Fridays were special for the Beavers. That was the day the Beaver offensive squad was required to run the opponents' scoring plays—the plays that a team most often uses from the 20-yard line in. The Beavers did their damnedest to score; and when Brian crossed the goal line, he made it look like the real thing. For that he voted himself the Beaver Player of the Year.

Brian had one complaint, in jest. Well, partly in jest. George Allen was the Bears' defensive coach that year. Chicago had won the National Football League Championship in 1963, largely due to his defensive squad, and Allen was justifiably proud of his men. Brian claimed that old George didn't like to see his boys embarrassed and for that reason wasn't reporting Piccolo's heroic efforts to the offensive coaches, the ones who held the key to Brian's future.

In the following years, after Brian had made the active squad, he and Ralph would stand on the sideline assessing the younger players. Few, they decided, could have made the Beaver team of old. Like battle veterans, football veterans develop a kind of arrogance.

Going into training camp in nineteen sixty-six I thought my chances were pretty good. Of course we had Andy Livingston and Gale, and the coaches were high on Andy. Joe Marconi was getting along in years, though, and Jon Arnett had announced his retirement. And then there were Ralphie and Ronnie Bull. They were both halfbacks and fullbacks; and I mention both because, although Halas had me pegged at halfback, my dream was to run in the same backfield with Gale; and that would put me right back at fullback, where I'd been in college, and where I felt I belonged.

In assessing the Bears running-back picture early in training camp in 1966, Chicago sportswriter Bill Jauss wrote: "Halas complimented rookie Brian Piccolo in his first contact experience as a pro in Saturday's scrimmage. He said, 'Piccolo ran 18 yards for a touchdown and also made runs, if I remember correctly, of 9 yards and 7 and 9 again and 6 and 3.' 'And Piccolo was in a tough spot last year' added quarterback Rudy Bukich, 'with Gale Sayers so fast and playing so well . . . but Piccolo could become a good back too.'"

Almost coincident with these conversations, Jon Arnett walked back into camp, unretired. Halas fined him $800 for arriving eight days late. Piccolo's prospects fell. Brian liked Jon Arnett:

As a rookie, Jon taught me more about my position than anyone, including the coaches.

Halas liked Arnett too. Jon alternated with Sayers throughout the '66 season, and Piccolo, although he made the active roster, was relegated to the bomb squads.

Actually, I carried the ball three times in my second year—twice against Atlanta, once against Green Bay. I was very disappointed. Arnett began having the usual troubles with the Old Man— he was sounding off. Rudy Bukich didn't even want to play, and by mid-season we were out of it. They should have been giving me and Larry Rakestraw more experience.

At the time I thought I was wasting those first two years. And I was really mad at the Bears. I wanted to go somewhere else. It didn't make sense that I hadn't played more my second year. I used to dream about what it would have been like to play for Vince Lombardi. I knew I was his kind of back, his kind of man. With Taylor and Hornung getting older, there might have been a chance for me there. Of course, the gold dusters, Donny An-

derson and Jim Grabowski, were both my vintage, so you never know.

All I could do was play like hell when I was in on the bomb squads. Kurek did the same thing. He has tremendous, tremendous desire—that's his secret. I never thought Ralph would make the cut when I saw him as a rookie, and it turned out he thought the same about me. It's been said a million times but nobody who hasn't been there realizes how important desire is in football. Nobody would go down under those kicks like Ralphie—just nobody. It really is suicidal, and there are a lot of guys who won't do it. So as a player you understand why that kind of guy sticks.

Other things are important in football, like emotion. If you're emotionally revved up to hit someone, you can. Basketball, for instance, is the opposite. You have to be cool to pop your shots.

Consistency, though, is the thing I look for in a player. If I'm the coach, I don't want a guy who's giving me ups and downs all the time. If a man is great one week and does nothing the next, I think this man should definitely be checked out. You win more with the guy who'll give you a good effort all the time. He may not be as great, but if you design a play to work a certain way, at least it will work more often.

It really bothered me during the sixty-six season when somebody who knew I played with the Bears introduced me, and the other person said, "Oh, are you a rookie?" after being with the team

*a couple of years. I guess pride is partly an evil,
but little things like that bothered me.*

It was traditional that following the final game
and before leaving Chicago to spend the Christmas holidays with their families in various parts
of the country, each player would have a meeting
with management to assess the season and collect
his final paycheck. In these years the final check
was usually a big one because the player often
drew just a living salary during the season and received the balance of his contract in December.
Also, during these years, the man the players often
met with was George Halas, their coach and, perhaps more significantly, their owner.

When Brian met with George Halas following
the '66 season, he told him how disappointed he
was that he had not been given more opportunity
to play. And he told the Old Man about his dream
of playing with Sayers.

*I told Coach Halas that I was going to start
pestering him to play fullback if Andy Livingston
didn't recover from that knee.* [Livingston had
had knee surgery following a preseason injury.] *I
had been sitting around quietly for two years
without getting a chance. I didn't know how effective it would be to pester Halas, but sitting
around saying nothing hadn't gotten me anywhere.*

Brian talked quite a bit during that off-season
about playing out his option and getting himself
traded. He even dreamed of jumping to the Amer-

ican League and maybe playing with the Miami Dolphins. But by now the two leagues had merged and there would be no interleague trading until 1970. Besides, Pic wasn't that discontented with the Bears, and in his less frustrated moments faced the situation realistically.

Anybody like me who played out his option would be playing himself right out of professional football.

To Brian, a man's opinion was only as valuable as the man himself. And one man he respected highly was his friend, all-pro middle linebacker Dick Butkus. Too bad Dick wasn't his coach.

"Sure, I'd put Pic in my starting backfield," Butkus said, in retrospect. "He had great hands and he was a good pattern man and he'd block for you. Some guys just won't. The Taylor-Hornung type combination would have been perfect for Pic. But the main thing about Brian was that he could find the holes and he ran with authority. I've tackled a lot of backs, and some go down easier than others. Size and speed are factors, but they're not everything. Pic ran low to the ground with his head up. That kind is hard to tackle. He was a money player, and he had confidence—all kinds of confidence."

Pic had more confidence than Butkus did on

the banquet circuit. Dick was in great demand for public appearances but, especially in the early years, he avoided all but the most lucrative opportunities. The fact was that whatever Dick lacked in confidence on the speaker's rostrum, he made up in authority. But in spite of himself, Butkus turned into a good public speaker, and he got a lot of help from Piccolo. He would often call Brian before an engagement to bum a couple of good one liners. Pic wouldn't come up with a thing without asking Dick what he was getting for the speech. Dick would tell him, "Oh, three hundred and fifty or so," and Brian would cringe. *Why in the hell should I be giving you material?* he'd say before giving Butkus just what he asked for.

Brian never got into the $300 bracket. That was for the "stars." Pic didn't resent the fact, but he sure as hell was envious.

Dick and Brian were a lot alike. They were alike in their dedication to football and alike in the essential strength and privacy of their personalities. But they were not alike in their prospects. Going into the '67 season, Dick Butkus had a fair chance of making first string.

As the Bears broke training camp, streaming north from Rensselaer, Indiana, to their homes in Chicago, Brian had a Bill Gleason column from the *Sun-Times* tucked in his shirt pocket. Bill had asked the coaches to assess their backfield talent. "How good is Piccolo? Well, this is his chance. He makes it this year or he doesn't and I think he knows that," Luke Johnsos had told Gleason. Luke was the Bears' head offensive coach.

Traditionally, the Chicago Bears home opener is the Armed Forces game, the final contest of the exhibition season; and their opponents during Piccolo's years were the St. Louis Cardinals who, until '59, were the South Side's Chicago Cardinals. Fan interest was high, Chicago still having a considerable number of latent Cardinal fans. Besides, with Wrigley Field being sold out for every game, mostly to season ticket holders, for many people this was the only chance to see the Bears in person. So although it was an exhibition match, the Armed Forces benefit game was not taken lightly.

Three things happened on that steamy Friday night in 1967 on Chicago's lakefront that pleased Pic: Gale had his best game of the exhibition period, scoring twice against the St. Louis Cardinals, once on a 70-yard run. Larry Rakestraw, in his first real chance in three years, started, played the entire first half, and left the field with the score 25-7 and an ovation ringing in his ears. And Piccolo was 30 for 10 on the ground and he caught two passes, one of them a spectacular touchdown snag in front of the Cardinals' All-Pro defensive back, Larry Wilson. Pic didn't need to star, he just liked a good showing. Besides, he liked the final score: 42-14.

During this season Brian and Gale had become roommates and began to establish the rapport that eventually led to a warm friendship.

Gale Sayers enjoyed special status with the Chicago Bears. His fellow players didn't quite know why, except, as the Old Man often said, "Gale is the greatest running back since Red Grange." For whatever reason, George Halas and his family established a close personal relationship with Gale and his wife, Linda. They mixed socially, something Halas rarely did with his players. Gale often told people, "George Halas is like a father to me." Gale's unusual position carried over to the practice field and into the games. Brian was one of the few people who refused to place his friend in a privileged role. On the field, the coach usually didn't take Gale in and out of games—Gale did.

Bill Bondurant, Pic's good friend and a writer from Fort Lauderdale, got it from Brian this way:

Sayers comes out after an offensive series. Piccolo goes over to him.

You want to take a blow, Gale? he asks.

"Yeah," Sayers replies.

Piccolo hunts up backfield coach Ed Cody on the sidelines. *Hey, Ed, Gale says he needs a blow.*

Cody dashes over to Sayers. "Gale, you really want to take a blow?"

"Yeah," Sayers gasps, this time for emphasis.

Cody rips over to Coach George Halas. "George, Gale says he needs a blow."

Halas looks around and crooks a finger. "Pic," he yells. "Get in there. Gale needs a blow."

After eight games of the '67 season, Ray Sons of the *Chicago Daily News* came up with some interesting information to substantiate Brian's inclusion in a list of the NFL's most versatile backs. Brian had 146 yards rushing and an even 100 in pass receptions. Sons observed that Piccolo was used extensively only in the Bears' three victories. In the team's five losses he hardly played at all.

Win or lose, there was still time for fun, and if there was anything Brian liked to do, it was eat. Unlike many other ballplayers, it wasn't volume that interested him, it was variety. Sometimes he would come out of one of his favorite restaurants and tell his companions:

That food almost made me cry, it was so good.

His favorite meal, Italian, naturally, was linguine and white clam sauce, and for years he had been telling his friends that no one could make it like he could. Finally, they challenged him to prove his boast. The party would be at the Kureks' in north suburban Deerfield, because the Piccolos' tiny house wouldn't accommodate all the guests. But Brian would do the cooking.

Preparations started early in the week when Brian called Kathy Kurek to find out what kind of kettles she had, which spices were in her cupboard, and how many burners were on the stove. Pic ended by bringing his own kettles—Kathy's weren't big enough—and Ralph found himself making last minute repairs on a faulty stove burner. Everything had to be perfect. There would be 10 for dinner on Thursday night: the Concannons, the Randy Jacksons, and the Mike Reillys would join the Kureks and the Piccolos.

The plan was that Brian would hitch a ride to practice on Thursday with Dick Butkus, who was the only other far South Sider on the team, and then go north to Deerfield with Ralph after work. Joy was to pick up the fresh clams and oysters (to be served on the half shell), load all the equipment in the station wagon, and meet Brian at the Kureks'. Then the fun would start. The following is Brian's recipe:

LINGUINE WITH WHITE CLAM SAUCE

    2 doz. fresh clams
    (Little Necks are the best,
        but if you have to get big ones,
        cut them up)
    ½ cup olive oil
    2 tsp. fresh chopped parsley
    ½ tsp. salt
    ¼ tsp. oregano
    1 clove garlic sliced thin
    pinch, hot pepper seed
    1 to 2 lb. linguine
        (depending upon how much
        sauce you like on it)

Be sure to have handy at least two large kettles and some cheesecloth (a diaper will do).
Scrub and clean clams with a good stiff brush. Put whole clams in frying pan, lid on, with a little water. They will steam open. Remove meat and

put in bowl. Strain the broth through cheese cloth.

Brown garlic in olive oil, add pepper seed, parsley, salt, and oregano. Add clam broth and clams to this mixture, and simmer for 30 minutes.

Bring water to boil in large kettle. Add linguine. Before linguine is done, transfer one to three ladles of linguine water into broth mixture according to taste. Add slowly.

Strain linguine *al dènte* (when it is firm to the tooth).

Serve with hot clam sauce in linguine bowls (they must be larger and flatter than soup bowls).

"But it seems it's not what you do, it's how you do it," Ralph reflected later. "Cooking with Brian was a ritual. And Pic has his dumb Polack friend —me—doing all the dirty work. I scrubbed six dozen clams and had to open six dozen oysters. We didn't even let the women in the kitchen. They had to mind the children. Brian said it was important to be undisturbed, and the kids should be kept quiet."

The men tore the kitchen apart, and then they feasted. Everyone agreed that Brian was right, it was one of the greatest meals anyone present had ever enjoyed. Brian never stopped smiling. Hadn't he told them?

The Bears finished 1967 with a record of seven wins, six losses, and one tie. The season ended with Gale moving the ball 880 yards on the ground for a 4.7 average and Piccolo finishing second with 317 yards and a 4.1 average per carry. A fan at a Chicago Quarterback Club banquet asked Coach Halas why he didn't play Sayers and Piccolo in the same backfield. "Sounds like a fine combination," the Old Man replied, politely. "We might try it . . . next year."

On May 27, 1968, the Chicago Bears called a press conference. George Halas announced his retirement after 50 years in professional football. In 1919, as a rookie outfielder for the New York Yankees, Halas had injured his hip sliding into third after hitting a triple off pitcher Rube Marquard. The injury ended his baseball ambitions and forced young George to pursue his second love, football. The hip had been bothering him ever since 1919, but now a new operation had been developed, and it looked like something could be done. Besides, the Old Man said, he couldn't run up and down the field anymore to keep within shouting distance of the officials. His decreased sideline activity not only frustrated Halas but disappointed the customers.

As for Piccolo, it tickled him to know that the Old Man, like himself, had been forced to give up baseball for football. Halas had found a degree of success in the game, so maybe there was hope for Brian too. But Pic had no idea what to expect from his new head coach, Jim Dooley, as the '68 season approached.

Training camp is miserable. I've always hated

it, and I always will. There you are at Saint Jo-
seph's College in Rensselaer, Indiana, and all you
can see for miles around is corn. Halas found
Rensselaer and Saint Joe's about a million years
ago and decided it was the perfect place for a
training camp. There are no distractions—and I
mean there are no distractions. Some of the great-
est stories the old vets ever tell are about the
lengths they went to in order to create distrac-
tions.

The idea is, I think, that in order to maintain
your sanity—in order to leave camp with the same
head you took in—you have to create your own
insanities. I don't think it would be the same if
we were located somewhere near our families or
other reasonable "distractions"; but at Rensselaer
that's the way it is. Nothing to do but work and
worry in all that heat, and when we play I guess
we play like kids. That's what the Old Man calls
everybody. "Kid." And he means it.

But the Bears have improved some since I've
been with the team. For instance, those of us
with a good enough excuse, like business, can
have a phone put in our rooms, so we don't have
to line up for the pay phone in the hall anymore.
Also we can go home on Saturdays now if no
game is scheduled. And they did away with the
ridiculous Halas Mile. Imagine me running a
mile the first day in camp. For crissake, it's only
ten yards to a first down. My rookie year was the
last for the mile. They also stopped timing us in
wind sprints that year. That was a relief. So far

I've made it through my entire career without anyone ever having put a stopwatch on me.

It was Brian's habit to send a postcard to Carol on every road trip from each town he visited during his football travels. Getting mail was a big event in her monotonous day, and she had scrapbooks full of Brian's picture postcards. During the summer of 1968, Carol received one from Rensselaer with a statue on the front. On the back Brian had written:

> *Dear Carol:*
> *I finally found a statue in Rensselaer. But it's so ugly the pigeons won't even shit on it.*
> *Love, Brian*

Everybody knows what football players do during training camp. They practice with the idea of getting into condition, which means grueling practice. They learn new plays. They worry about getting cut or traded or injured. Some just think about getting out of practice. But the only way to get out of practice is to get cut or traded or injured.

Many ballplayers turn to pranks for amusement. The schedule, tension, and schoolboy disciplinary systems they work under at training camp encourage such behavior. During Brian's years, men came out of liberal college environments, where responsibility and self-sufficiency were expected of them, and were thrust into a restrictive atmosphere unknown since early child-hood. A man had to make the best of it.

Probably the most popular way for the players to spend their scattered leisure hours was the same way the townsfolk spent their time: just driving around or sitting in a few of the local spots and socializing.

One thing that both appalled and awed Ralph was Brian's habit of pulling the car over and talking to just about anybody—about anything. "Brian just enjoyed people enjoying him." There was one occasion that stuck in Ralph's mind.

"One day we saw this little girl on a street corner, and she was twirling a baton, and she was pretty good; not only that, she was pretty good-looking. We had seen her in years past with the baton, but now she was about thirteen and she'd changed a lot, as girls will. Brian insisted on pulling over. And he started talking to her, asking her how long she'd been working with the baton—things like that. As he was talking I could see the expression on the girl's face. She just started bubbling. Pretty soon her father came out, and they all carried on a conversation, with the little girl still the center of attention. I'll never forget Brian's parting words. He said, *'I'm going to be going down to a Purdue game in a couple of years, and I plan to see you on the field at half time. You will be Purdue's Golden Girl.'* It was all he had to say. You could tell from her face that being Purdue's Golden Girl had been her dream."

Bob Wetoska, the Bears' veteran tackle, started out like Brian did, on the taxi squad. In the best tradition of pro football, Bob was a man of great integrity and an inveterate fun lover. Every year, toward the end of training camp, he gave a party. One of Dick Butkus's favorite contests took place at training camp in 1965, when he and Brian were rookies together. Wetoska's Annual Party, to be held in Rensselaer's pizza parlor, was coming up, and the rookies were anxiously waiting to see if they'd be invited. They were. "I ate dinner first," said Butkus. "You've got to before one of these things. And when I got over there some of the guys were well on their way. After a while the veterans decided that we rookies would have a chugging contest. My managers were Ed O'Bradovich and Richie Petitbon. I don't know how much money Rich and OB laid around on me, but there was a lot of it in sight. Anyhow, this Piccolo was really swaggering. He told everybody he could beat me, and I guess he had such a big mouth some of the guys believed him. Well, he made a good show. But hell, I could have beaten him drinkin' through a straw. It didn't look like he'd ever tried to chug beer before in his life. I don't know if they had beer in that North Carolina town where he went to school. They sure had it at Illinois."

The most satisfying time killer at training camp

was taunting the Spy. The Spy was an ordinary citizen of Rensselaer, but the players endowed him with all kinds of sinister characteristics. However, the Spy did indeed make detailed reports to the Bear management about the players' off-hour activities.

A look out the window of the dorm after hours would show the Spy in his old green Dodge, checking the parking lot. It was easy to note an absence, because each player's car was assigned a specific parking slot for just that purpose.

It was a big thing to keep track of the Spy. Brian and Ralph loved to get him to follow them. With Brian driving Ralph's more maneuverable Triumph, they would tie the Spy in knots, taking him to places only Brian's imagination could lead them. The challenge was to see if they could double back and end up following the Spy. Actually, it wasn't very hard to do.

To the players, the Spy was a joke, a diversion, objected to more on principle than on practical grounds. The men would wave to him as they entered and left the Wagon Wheel, a tavern just down the road from St. Joe's and a good place for a postpractice beer.

The Great Stoning Incident was warmly satisfying to several players, notably Brian Piccolo. The Spy was sitting one evening at his usual parking lot observation post, when several men, armed with bags of nonlethal paraphernalia, crept onto the dormitory roof and began bombing the Spy. From all reports, the man didn't know what hit him or from where. And the perpetrators still believe themselves to be anonymous.

What makes such behavior fun for grown men is the risk involved. Had they been caught, it would have cost each of them a pocketful of cash, maybe $500. In the days when a man's allowance for camp was $10 a day, for a broken rule or two he would end up owing money to the Old Man.

There were all kinds of ways to enjoy life, but in Rensselaer you really had to work at it. Fortunately, training camp didn't last forever.

It turned out that Jim Dooley was a great innovator. He designed what he called the "total offense," which looked good to me, because in some formations Gale was at flanker, with Bull and me as setbacks. Dooley even brought back the old tight T with three running backs. I figured, particularly with Gale loosening up defenses at flanker, we'd all three of us average five yards a carry in the sixty-eight season. And we'd all be happy.

The Bears' 1968 total offense was "totaled," the first two games of the season, 38-28 by the Washington Redskins and 42-0 by the Detroit Lions. It took the fans exactly one game to find out that with the new coach, Jim Dooley, the Bears still had their historic "quarterback problem." Starter Concannon was yanked after the first series of the second half and replaced by Larry Rakestraw. The quarterback had been the scapegoat for years with the Bears. The shifting of quarterbacks not only created mechanical difficulties for the offensive players but the whole team suffered a setback in morale. Piccolo did his share to keep things lively.

Hey, Super Nigger, you gonna work today? You trying to kill the Dago, or what?

Brian Piccolo was directing his remarks to Gale Sayers, who was standing by during a practice session at Wrigley Field.

There was no malice intended by Brian and none taken by Gale. Brian was a true believer in the richness of racial and ethnic heritages. He was damned proud of being an Italian and loved Dago jokes. Brian expected Concannon to be proud of his Boston-Irish background and Kurek to boast of his Polish farming family; he knew Gale was proud to be black. And somehow Brian could always make his humor work for the good of the team. The Lord knew the Bears needed everything they could get going for them early in the season, even Piccolo's perverse flippancy.

Brian was mild mannered and, unlike some of his peers, slow to rile on the football field. But Bob Wetoska remembered one instance when Brian did lose his temper; it was during a game in which a referee made a call that Pic disagreed with—violently. Pic stormed up to the official, who had a very Italian name, and he sputtered for a few seconds before he hissed in the official's face:

You couldn't be a Dago . . . you're a . . . a Polack.

Wetoska, a purebred Pole, roared at that one.

Dick Butkus was Polish too, and reared on Chicago's South Side. Brian had learned to respect the South Siders: they were a special breed themselves. Brian, though, was truly awed by his teammate Butkus. Gale and Brian often sat together on the bench when the defense was in, just watching Butkus work.

Dick, Brian said, *is the most complete football player I have ever known. He has so much desire and likes to hit so much that he destroys ballcarriers. He doesn't just tackle them, he sort of picks them up and drives them back. Then he throws them down on their backs hard, and as the guy is bouncing off the ground, Butkus comes down on him full force. It's nothing dirty, it's just the way he tackles. Sometimes, after a really hard one, Gale and I look at each other out of reflex. We're thankful he plays for us.*

The '68 season was destined to be a wild one for the Bears. Butkus's tackles would mean a lot. Going into the sixth game they had lost four and won one, and the players had worked with quarterbacks Rakestraw, Rudy Bukich, and Jack Concannon, who had broken his collarbone in the midst of an impressive performance that resulted in the season's first victory against Minnesota. Concannon's injury caused the elevation from the taxi squad of quarterback Virgil Carter, two years out of Brigham Young University and barely seasoned. But Carter, with a lot of help, particularly from place-kicker Mac Percival, led the Bears to four victories in a row. Against Green Bay, Piccolo played well in relief, especially in the pass-receiving department. Brian had his best days when Gale was in top form, because the more long runs Magic made, either on kickoff returns or from scrimmage, the more his sub was used to give him a rest. Sayers scampered like someone inspired against the Packers, carrying 24 times for 205 yards.

But during their victory over the 49ers in the eighth game of the season, defensive back Kermit Alexander struck Magic a clean blow, and Gale was out for the season with a "total rupture of all ligaments on the inside of the right knee and torn cartilage." It was the football player's nightmare, and for Magic a frightening setback. But his friend Pic wasn't worried about him. Pic was used to setbacks, and he knew they could be overcome. Meanwhile, cruel as the circumstances were, Gale's nightmare meant Pic's dream had come true. He would start for the Chicago Bears.

"You couldn't really say Pic could run," said Jack Concannon, "but he always did the job. Being a football player and saying it was pleasant to work with someone sounds, well, freaky. But it was the truth. When I'd call a play where the ball would go to Brian, you could just see that grin come over his face. He'd look at me—and it was beautiful."

So Brian started in the ninth game of the '68 season, three years after he had entered the NFL. He caught seven passes for 92 yards in the next game against Atlanta. Unfortunately, however, a linebacker named Tommy Nobis crashed into his quarterback, Virgil Carter, and Virg didn't get up. His ankle was broken. So the Bears lost the game and another quarterback. Brian sprained his ankle the following week as the Bears went under to the Cowboys. His leg was swollen and ugly, but now that Piccolo was where he wanted to be, he was going to stay there.

They'd have to tear both my legs off to get me out now, Brian said.

The doctor shot Pic's ankle full of cortisone and novocaine, and against the New Orleans Saints the following week the Bears won 23-17, Piccolo carrying 21 times for 112 yards.

After being defeated by Dallas, a headline had read, "Bears Experiment for Future," indicating the season was lost. Then, following the New Orleans victory, Dick Butkus spoke the unbelievable words: "Now we can win it all." The task was simple, clear-cut: Just beat Los Angeles, which was going down to the wire with Baltimore in the Coastal Division and had to win, and then beat the Green Bay Packers, who had a chance at the Central Division title themselves, should Chicago and Minnesota lose. It was one of those years.

> "It would be nice to beat George Allen."
>> *George Halas*
>> *George Halas, Jr.*
>> *Jim Dooley and the entire*
>> *Bear coaching staff*

The odds makers favored the Rams; it would have been a bad bet. The Bears beat George Allen's Rams with Ronnie Bull and Piccolo punching out the yards on the ground and Concannon, now fully recovered from his broken collarbone, leading a ball-control attack. A big share of the credit had to go to the Bears' defense, which held Ram quarterback Roman Gabriel to only eight completions in 26 attempts, while the Rams' Fearsome Foursome never penetrated the Bears' offensive line to touch Concannon. Everybody worked and worked hard for the 17-16 victory.

> *No matter what, the fans are going to remember this season. Who'd have thought we'd still be in it now?*
>> *Brian Piccolo*

On December 14th, as Green Bay and Chicago met for the 100th time, the thermometer stood well below freezing, and the wind blew at 16 miles an hour from the northwest corner of Wrigley Field. This was "Packer weather." And the Bears lost, 28-27, to wind up one of the most

BRIAN PICCOLO

erratic, exciting, misfortune-studded seasons in
their history.

"What the hell, wait till next year."
                    Almost every athlete,
                    almost every year

"It was kind of a mystery to me," said Ed
McCaskey. "At the end of each season the
coaches would say, 'You know, our highest
rated back is Piccolo. Piccolo never makes
a mistake. Piccolo carries out every assignment given him perfectly. You never have to
explain to Piccolo more than once.' And I
could never understand why they couldn't
find a way to play this man more than they
did if this was the case.

*After what I did in sixty-eight I felt I should be
playing regular, not just waiting around for the
coaches to take Gale out and put me in. I gained
four hundred and fifty yards in six games. I honestly believe that carrying the ball ten or fifteen
times a game and playing regularly, I could gain
a thousand yards a year. But when Gale's in
there, they want him to carry seventy-five percent
of the time. He doesn't mind that, and I don't
blame him. But I figured that if we went back
to that style of play in sixty-nine, Gale would
have another great year, and the Bears would
finish seven-seven again—or maybe eight-six. I
was wrong—Gale broke a thousand yards, a great*

-140

achievement, but the team finished one-thirteen.

It wasn't until after the sixty-eight season that I had my first taste of contract hassle. I had never asked for a multi-year or no-cut contract for the simple reason that I wanted to be rewarded if I had a real good season. Sixty-eight was pretty decent for me. I came within one catch of leading the team in pass receptions, just playing part-time. Of course that doesn't say much for our passing game. I caught twenty-eight.

I didn't want to get into it with the Halases over contract. Hell, the Old Man was my knight in shining armor. He's the one who gave me a chance. But there are some things that should weigh in a contract that just don't. I think if a guy's a good guy, doesn't cause you problems, if he works for the team and runs down on kickoffs without bitching about it—these things should be considered. The club would be happier.

Consider the linemen. I think every backfield man should play on the line sometime during his career, because it really makes you appreciate what it's like in the pit. It's a whole new world. And my experience was just in high school; I can imagine what it's like in the pros. These guys get beat up more than anybody, and they get so little recognition. And they've got to be the lowest on the pay scale.

It is one of the great inequities of pro ball. Maybe I, if I was an owner, I'd do the same thing. But I don't think so. It seems like someday they should sit down and start paying the guys accord-

*ing to what the hell they do. They should ask
how much does a man contribute when I put him
in there? Not how much does he contribute when
I don't, because obviously the guy hasn't got a
chance. That's always the big argument for so
many of the guys, just as it was for me earlier in
my career: When you don't have a chance to
prove what you can do, you don't have anything
to bargain with.*

*I tried to make my position clear going into
the sixty-nine season. I wanted to play, and I
wanted a reasonable raise, and we settled our
differences, and I signed. I didn't give any ultimatums. Ultimatums don't work so well with the
Bears.*

"For three years," said Joy, "every time
he'd bring his playbook home I knew the
coaches had told him he might be going in
at fullback on Sunday. But it didn't happen
until it was too late."

The Bears played Los Angeles in the sixth
game of the '69 season. Brian Piccolo was still
backing up Sayers but had been carrying the ball
in practice from the fullback slot. All three quarterbacks—Concannon, Carter, and now the rookie,
Bobby Douglass, from Kansas—had been trotted
out. The Rams handed the Bears their sixth loss
and sent fullback Ronnie Bull off the field with
a knee injury. Piccolo was first string again. His
ambition was realized, and next week against the

Vikings he would run in tandem with Sayers. But Pic had developed a cough and wasn't feeling well.

Nevertheless, against Minnesota, Brian carried seven times for 37 yards and a 5.3 average, while Magic carried 20 for 116 and a 5.8 average. Those stats were all right. But the Bears lost 31-14. Coach Jim Dooley told the gathered press: "We can't go on like this. But I don't know what changes will be made until I evaluate the films." His statement reminded one reporter of the time he had gone into an NFL office and immediately spotted a young coach who was a recent bridegroom. "How was the honeymoon, George?" asked the reporter. "I don't know," the coach replied, "I'll talk to you after I evaluate the films."

Everyone had just about forgotten what winning felt like when the Bears beat Pittsburgh 38-7 in Wrigley Field on November 9th. Pic was beginning to have a hard time breathing, but he carried the ball 12 times for 31 yards and caught two passes for 20 yards and one touchdown.

It's hell to lose all the time. It's just plain hell to be in that bag. Things seem to fall apart, and it's hard to understand why, and it's even harder to know just what will turn you around. It was good to beat Pittsburgh, even if they didn't have the greatest team in the league. There's nothing that gets you up like a win. I wasn't feeling too red hot, and the trainer didn't seem to be doing anything for my cough, but I was ready and really looking forward to going to Atlanta and playing the Falcons and visiting with Herb and Grace and Carol. Hell, I wouldn't have traded my life up to that point with anybody.

It's a glorious way to make a buck. Don't ever believe it isn't. Hell, I'd play for nothin'. I'm not going to tell Halas that, but I'd play football for nothin'.

That's why it was so hard to hear those words— so hard to listen to Dr. Beattie say: "You will never be able to play football again."

Ed McCaskey and Gale Sayers had been there all afternoon the first of April. It had been one week since Brian's mastectomy. Brian's cough was getting bad again, and it was hard for him to talk. It was raining outside, one of those dull days. As usual Ed and Gale were playing everything for laughs, but this time they were silly. Joy was living with Max and Dorothy Kendrick now; however, Joy was at the hospital throughout the day, which forced the men to sanitize their repartee. That wasn't the whole problem, though. His friends could see a change in Brian, and they were frightened. Their humor was edged with tension.

It was a relief when a nurse came in and commented that Brian had needed a lot of blood and would they care to donate some to make up part of the deficit. A history of hepatitis made Ed ineligible, so he volunteered to go out for an Italian dinner—a change of pace from the hospital cuisine. In the meantime, Ed said, Magic could hang around and bank a pint or two. Gale said okay, his blood was the same type as Brian's.

A few days later Brian was telling everyone that since Gale had given him some blood, *I've developed this tremendous craving for chitlins.*

Ed returned from his forage loaded down with parmigiana and spaghetti and soaking wet. He took off his shirt and hung it up to dry. Ed and Gale did most of the eating while Brian gave Joy her 500 millionth lecture about putting on some weight.

Food and paper and Coke bottles were all over the room when Dr. Beattie walked in with his entourage. It was an anxious moment for Ed. Beattie gave him the high sign to move into the hall for a word, and Ed figured he was going to get hell for being half naked in Beattie's hospital. But all Beattie said to Ed was, "Please see me in my office tomorrow."

Ed was filled with dread the next morning. He knew the news would not be good. Beattie started out by saying that he had never had a patient with whom he had become more emotionally involved than he had with Brian. "He is like a son to me and Joy is like my daughter." ("Which was a relief," Ed said later. "I noticed he had been hugging her a lot.") "But," the doctor said, "Brian's left lung will have to come out." He felt that the cancer was confined to the chest, and if he could get the lung clean there was still a chance. He was planning to tell Brian his evaluation that afternoon.

Ed got Gale alone and told him. They were both devastated at the thought of Pic taking another blow, right on top of the mastectomy. Pic's two friends were in the room when Dr. Beattie came in and announced to Brian that they had to talk. Ed asked if they should leave, but Brian said,

No, there's nothing you can't hear.

Then Beattie told him: The lung would have to come out. He would never be able to play football again. Dr. Beattie said,

"Brian, it's there—it's got to come out. I'd like to take it this weekend." Brian chuckled strangely and said,

No! No, I'm not ready for it, my mind is not ready for it. Let's wait.

Dr. Beattie said, "Okay."

The first thing Brian said when Joy and Dorothy walked in was, *You've been crying, Joy.*

She had. Joy always got the bad news first. Brian's voice was breaking.

I'll never play football again, and I've known it all along; but to hear it put into words is another thing. Really, Joy, I've known it.

He too began to cry, and Dorothy left them alone together.

What does a football player do who can't play football? I think I fulfilled my real ambition in pro football. My idea of success is to be established, to know that I could play for almost anybody, to have the respect around the league of other players and coaches. This I felt I had accomplished. Of course, I didn't plan on having it end this soon.

Now. Well, I have to build on this. I was just past the point of beginning. Many pro athletes don't know what they want because they want so much. I've always felt that no matter whom you're dealing with or what you're dealing with, you should pretty well decide what it would take to make you happy in a particular deal. Anything over and above it is cream. If you get what you want, you should be happy about it.

The biggest problem most pro athletes have is that they're always looking out other windows. For example, if a guy signs a contract with the Bears and he hears that a certain guy at his position is getting ten grand more with some other team, all of a sudden he is moaning instead of thinking about football. It affects his play and his attitude toward the club. Half the time the information is bullshit anyhow. I remember one of my biggest thrills was when I worked out a deal for a car—a few appearances to drive a new demonstrator for a year. I thought I'd finally arrived.

The thing is, I don't like training camp. I don't like practice. But competition, the game, it's glorious. You're doing something you love. I don't believe there is enough money in the world to make a guy play football just for the money. He'd have to like it. I can't comprehend a guy thinking: "Well, I'll play two more years and make fifty thousand dollars more and save so much. . . ." Going through training camp with nothing but that motivation would be impossible.

The first thing a guy's got to have is determination, because so many times, when you think about it, a man's career is such a long road. I started on my road when I was eight and I got to pro ball when I was twenty-one. There were so many ups and downs it was unbelievable. You've got to believe in yourself. Not to show anybody else—because who gives a damn what anybody else thinks?—but just to prove it to yourself.

Sure a guy's got to have some talent. Determination, talent, and a lot of luck. You have to be in the right place at the right time. In my case, I happened to be a running back, and they happened to draft Gale Sayers the same year. Now, that's not exactly the best way to bust into the league. That's not what you'd call being in the right place at the right time.

The Chicago Bears decided in 1967 to integrate

roommates on the road. The idea was to room the players by position. Ed Cody, the backfield coach, approached Gale at training camp just before a scheduled trip to Birmingham for an exhibition game. "Gale," he said, "I'm going to room you with Ronnie Bull." "Why Bull?" Gale asked. Gale wasn't color-blind, he knew some big deal was in the works. "We've just decided to room backs together," said Cody. "Okay," Gale replied, "but give me Piccolo." Gale said later that it was just instinct that made him say "Piccolo." He didn't know Brian real well. But he knew Pic was a kidder, as lighthearted as he was light skinned.

Nobody asked Brian whom he wanted. He found out when Gale walked into his room. (Sometime later Pic got off one of his more infamous remarks: *Hell, I don't mind rooming with Sayers, as long as he doesn't use the bathroom.*)

Gale soon discovered he'd made a good choice.

"There was something about Brian. I don't know what it was. But he could call you a Nigger and you'd know—*you'd know*—he was kidding. Sometimes we made other people uncomfortable, the way we talked, because they thought even if we were just kidding, it wasn't very funny. But it was funny to us. A black guy on the team, he can call anybody a Nigger, but Pic was the only white guy could get by with it.

"Sixty-nine was such a bad year. Before one of the games, Paul Patterson was walking around on the practice field giving little pep talks to all the black players. Paul's sort of assigned to us. Anyhow, Piccolo's following Paul all over the field riding him: 'What are you going to do for the Italians, huh, Paul? Why don't we have a rep? How come the Niggers get all the attention? You prejudiced against Italians, Paul?' We never had much of a racial problem on the Bears, and Pic went about it ass backwards, but he really made things better.

"When Bennie McRae became our first black captain, Pic figured he would take all his grievances to Bennie. Since he was my roommate, Brian told Bennie, that qualified him as a soul brother.

"Pic never bad mouthed anybody. They say people who like themselves like other people, and Brian was never short on self-confidence. He truly liked people. But he was sarcastic as hell. He'd get you that way. After we started playing together, he would get to me pretty good if I missed a block.

"The first time I saw Brian after his original operation was Sunday, December sixth. I flew into Chicago from San Francisco, where we'd played, changed planes, and went right on to New York. Pic was in a beautiful mood. Really something. He was walking around. Showed me his scar, he was very proud of his scar, you know. It went from his neck almost to his navel and then across his left side below the sternum. He couldn't help reminding me how rotten I'd been after my first knee operation. *'Want to compare scars?'* he'd say.

"But after the second operation, the mastectomy, he wasn't so proud. He had this great patch over his breast, and he showed me where it was missing and he said, *'Magic, ain't this a bitch. Look at me.'* But the change was just physical. His spirits were great. I felt like he was fighting for his sanity with his wild sense of humor, because every day he could see he was deteriorating."

Much had been made of Brian's friendship with Gale, of the fact that they were roommates. The situation had some built-in dramatics.

The fact is that Sayers and Piccolo didn't exactly fall all over each other with joy on becoming roommates. Brian, after all, was a southern boy, although his dominant goodwill toward all people seemed to negate any latent prejudice. And on paper, at least, Gale was his competitor at halfback.

Gale, although he is a man with little natural suspicion, certainly understood the realities of being a black man. He had some apprehension. But Magic and Pic had two things in common: open minds and open hearts. They became friends. Two accidents of fate, though, Gale's knee injury and Brian's illness, brought them closer together.

Brian got his first chance to start when Gale injured his knee. And yet, Gale said, while the fans and the press were skeptical, Brian was the one man who never lost confidence in his ability to come back. Pic consistently encouraged him, whether it was during his off-season rehabilitation, at film sessions, or on the field.

Brian had a gay, effusive personality; inside he was cool and introspective. Gale appears distant to some people, shy to others; privately he is warm and affectionate. Gale has said he has had three close friends and Brian was one of them.

Gale and I got acquainted our second year. We lockered according to numbers: forty, Sayers; forty-one, Piccolo; forty-five, Dick Gordon. I used to tell 'em they made me feel like an Oreo cookie.

When they made us roommates, we were forced to spend more time together. We roomed together three years, sixty-seven, sixty-eight, and sixty-nine. At first we didn't go out to eat together. When we'd get to a town, I'd call Ralphie or someone, and he'd call the guys he'd been hanging out with, and we'd split. Then we took to to going out in a big integrated bunch. Eventually it got to where Gale and I would always go out together, kind of rely on one another, you know. We'd talk about the game, individuals, most everything.

We'd talk a lot. I guess you could say we had something to learn from each other. Gale was working on his autobiography, his "life story" for crissake! I gave him a pretty bad time. We'd lie in bed at night and think up titles. He ended up calling it I am Third, *but my favorite was* Super Shine.

No doubt Gale was The Big Star. I never hesitated to tell him when I thought he did something wrong on the field, something most people, including the coaches, usually didn't do. When I'd call him for not running out a pattern or blocking, he'd just . . . agree.

There was no reason for anything I'd say to bother him. Possibly there should have been some competition between us. But there really was none. It was cut-and-dried. Gale was going to play. Actually, that made it easier. No way could I fight for the job, although I would always joke about it.

I knew he'd come back after the knee, mostly because of the way he worked it during the off-season. I never saw a guy so determined to get a thing back in shape. The real convincer was when he came back in sixty-eight. He never put a piece of tape on it, not even in practice. I never saw a guy come off a knee injury where he didn't wrap it. Gale persuaded himself he was one hundred percent.

I never resented Gale, he's a helluva athlete and a helluva man. But I did resent the coaches for not playing me with him. Nobody likes to beat his head against a stone wall.

Dr. Beattie once said, "A guy like Brian, he can

take a hard tackle, but being knocked down over and over again, that starts to wear on him."

The pneumonectomy on April 9th took hours. Dorothy waited with Joy. From seven o'clock in the morning until Dr. Beattie came to them at four in the afternoon, they heard nothing. "He is fine," the doctor said, but he added something about "iodine seeds . . . precautionary . . . took some extra time." Joy went with Dr. Beattie to visit Brian in intensive care. Brian's smile was magnificent when the doctor told him, "There will be no more surgery."

And then Brian was delivered into the hands of the radiotherapists.

HOSPITAL COURSE:

It was felt that an attempt should be made to remove the tumor from the left chest. He was taken to the operating room on 4/9/70. Bronchoscopy showed some distortion, but no intrinsic cancer was seen. A left pneumonectomy was performed. The tumor had extended through the pleura in the region of the left second rib. Additionally, there was a 3-4 cm. tumor in the supra-aortic area. Both areas were implanted by Dr. Hilaris. Twenty-four seeds were placed through 18 needles with a total dose of 12 mcs. The lesion in the medial anterior diaphragm was completely excised. The Marlex mesh which had previously been used to repair the large defect in the pericardium was adherent to the pericardium and coronary vessels and had some residual tumor along it. The plan was to use external radiotherapy postoperatively.

He convalesced well.

On 4/16/70 he received 1 mg of actinomycin-d, IV. After that, Dr. Golbey felt chemotherapy should be held off pending completion of the radiation therapy. Then a new protocol of chemotherapy should be used.

On 4/15/70, Dr. Hilaris began radition therapy to his chest wall lesion and approximately one week later, radiation to the mediastinum and the rest of the left region of the xiphoid. On 4/24/70, he was discharged to the Winston Apartment House to continue his radiation therapy as an outpatient.

During this time a lesion appeared near his xiphoid. A total dose of 1,000 rads to the mediastinum and left chest was given, and 3,500 rads to the xiphoid area. This was completed on 5/14/70. He returned to Chicago on 5/23/70.

FINAL DIAGNOSIS:
Malignant teratoma of mediastinum, postoperative; metastatic as embryonal cell carcinoma to left lung, pleura, and mediastinum, postoperative; metastatic to left pectoral muscle and axilla, postoperative; subcutaneous metastasis near xiphoid, suspected.

Probably the thought behind discharging Brian and letting him go through the course of radiotherapy as an outpatient was to get him out of the hospital atmosphere and to let Brian and Joy enjoy some time together. In actuality it didn't work out that way. Brian was exhausted and depressed through the full four weeks he spent at the Winston, across the street from the hospital.

There was more bite than wit to his conversation —when he talked. It was as though he was turning all his thoughts and energy inward, willing his disease to die, willing himself to live. At times he gave the impression that he was controlling a grand play of emotion. At other times he was simply drained—of everything.

He would leave the Winston apartment, but not often. The doctors had told Joy to force Brian to get out and walk. Joy had a good laugh at that one. She had never been able to "force" Brian to do anything. Sometimes other people could aid in her campaign. Tucker could get Brian as far as Mr. Laffs once in a while.

Visitors—and there were many those weeks at the Winston—saw the best Pic could muster. He put out for his friends. Some of them were, of course, in show business. A lot of people have said about comedians Phil Foster and Shecky Greene, "I laughed so hard I thought I'd die." Well, Brian didn't say it, but he just about did it. Gale and Ed came into town one evening and brought along Shecky, who had just finished an engagement in Chicago, and Eli Shulman. Eli has a restaurant on Chicago Avenue, and although it isn't exactly Italian, Brian was crazy about the place and about Eli. Ed called up Phil Foster when he got to New York. They all picked up Max and Dorothy Kendrick. After a delicious French dinner that Brian had declined, they trooped to the Winston to cheer the Piccolos.

Immediately, Phil and Shecky stationed themselves at Brian's feet and began to tell stories. Most of the material wasn't the standard night-club stuff—it was more personal. A couple of tales really grabbed Pic.

Phil Foster recounted a time, years before, when he and Buddy Hackett were both on their way to clubs in the Catskills. They drove up together and soon began noticing the killed deer strapped to many of the cars traveling the other way. It began to bug them, seeing those deer. So they got out in the next town and looked for a fish market. They bought the biggest fish they could find and tied it to the top of their car. Then they found a sporting goods store and bought a couple of arrows and stuck them in the fish. They drove happily off into the sunset, blowing the horn at the deer hunters, smug as hell. Pic wished he'd done that—what a great thing to do.

Then Phil launched into the story of how he had met Ed McCaskey. Ed and Phil had been assigned to the 66th Infantry Division at Camp Rucker in Alabama during World War II. Ed brought along his Irish Setter, Molly. (Ed has always been, in Brian's words, *A big dog man.*) Anyhow, Ed was chasing Molly down the street one afternoon, when he heard a voice drawl, "Hey, Lieutenant, you'll never catch that dog." Ed looked around and here was an enlisted man, lounging in a doorway, with his cap on crooked and his shirt collar open. Being a brand-new second lieutenant, Ed took umbrage and said, "How dare you speak to me that way? Come to attention. Salute!" Well, it was Foster, and he said, "Naw, go get three more." Ed said, "What do you mean, three more?" "Three more second lieutenants," Foster replied. "I only salute if there's four of you guys." McCaskey and Foster have been friends ever since.

Brian called George Halas often, just to assure the old man that he felt fine. He wanted to call Halas that night, so Ed placed the call, and everyone took turns with the phone. Shecky monopolized it, though. He started telling stories to the Old Man. But soon it became obvious that Brian had laughed himself into exhaustion. The entertainment troop left. Brian and Joy were alone again in the tiny apartment.

It was a great break in routine. But, for the most part, every day was the same for Brian. Each morning at 10:00 A.M. he would walk across 67th Street to the Firestone Pavillion, where Memorial kept one of its major weapons: cobalt.

The lobby looks like, well, say the lobby of a Hilton Inn. You know, blond woodwork and cheery modern furniture. You walk up over this curving ramp and turn left to an elevator which is slower than the second coming of Christ. On the second floor you hand the paper they gave you the day before to the girl at the appointment desk. She assigns you to an individual dressing room where you undress, however much your particular area requires. And then you wait.

There are four machines, and each treatment

lasts two minutes; but these machines go all day, five days a week. The other people waiting? I guess you try not to look at them. I mean it's a peculiar cross section—all quiet. Once there was an old, old man lying like a baby in a crib. And I remember a prosperous looking guy in his forties, perfectly okay except for these scarlet scars on his bald head. One person was hard to ignore—a dark skinned little girl, a little older than Lori, maybe five, and smiling all the time, with just a pigtail left to show the world she was a regular little girl. I guess she got it in the head too.

The room, when it's finally your turn, is totally dominated by the Machine. And somebody with a rotten sense of humor, or I guess, maybe a futile desire to please, has covered one wall with a huge mural. There are murals in all the rooms, and they sort of fight with the Machine for attention, you know. And they always lose. I can never figure out if this one mountain is Shasta or Kilimanjaro or Fuji. Maybe that's part of the psychology.

Anyhow, I know the position well now: Flat on my back so the Machine has a good shot at what's left of my breast and shoulder. Hell, the Machine scares me, and the picture makes me mad, so I guess I just glaze my eyes and try not to see anything.

The technician is always cheerful, and I'm pretty polite too. You learn that. She aims the monster at the red square, and then she leaves, kind of quickly, I've noticed. Cobalt produces gamma rays, which are just strong X rays. They act like regular light rays. They can be concentrated, but a certain amount of them diffuses, and they're not good for you unless you're sick—you dig? I mean it's downright ominous. There is this television camera in the room. You could see it if you turned. But the technician is watching you through that electronic eye, and if you move even slightly she's on you in a flash. She sits out there in front of this incredible space-center-type television monitor and instrument panel. She controls the camera, and she controls the Machine.

You know when she activates the Machine, because you can hear the low hum, but you feel nothing except fear or nausea. I'm never sure which is which. And then it is all over. Zap! The gal is through the lead door, and you're up and out and dressed and reaching for tomorrow's appointment slip and walking to that unbelievable slow elevator and through the lobby and down the ramp and across the street back to the Winston. I walk pretty slow. Concannon calls it the Piccolo shuffle, but sometimes the fresh air is great. I usually read the New York Times *for awhile, see how far I can get through the sports page before I fall asleep . . . I just fall asleep.*

That was cobalt. It was to have lasted four weeks, but the doctors decided to cut it to three. The radiation was completed on the 14th, and Brian and Joy went home on May 23rd.

Floridians and Southern Californians never get a chance to know what May is. Brian, who spent his youth in the bland Florida sunshine, learned after his first midwestern winter to appreciate the miracle of spring. The tulips were blooming in front of the house on Hunt Place as Joy and Brian arrived. The sky was blue, the new leaves green—as only new leaves can be—the breeze fresh. The beauty of his home was so great that Brian wanted to consume it in great gulps.

The plan was to spend a week at home and take care of the paper work, pay some bills, rest, and visit with friends. And then, right before Memorial Day, Brian and Joy would board a plane for Atlanta and visit their daughters for the first time in nine weeks.

On the same day the Piccolos returned home, Gale left for New York to accept the George S. Halas Award as the most courageous player in pro football for the '69 season. Gale had earned the trophy for rushing more than 1,000 yards in his comeback after knee surgery. But Gale had other ideas. As he received the award from George Halas in front of the hundreds of men gathered at the Professional Football Writers annual dinner, Gale turned and told the people in the audience that they had given their prize to the wrong man—that the most courageous man in football was Brian Piccolo.

> "He has the heart of a giant and that rare form of courage that allows him to kid himself and his opponent—cancer. He has the mental attitude that makes me proud to have a friend who spells out the word 'courage' twenty-four hours a day of his life. You flatter me by giving me this award, but I tell you that I accept it for Brian Piccolo. It is mine tonight, it is Brian Piccolo's tomorrow . . . I love Brian Piccolo, and I'd like all of you to love him too. Tonight, when you hit your knees, please ask God to love him . . ."

Dr. Beattie was at the banquet, sitting with Ed McCaskey. They cried. The entire audience at the stag affair was shaken.

Brian found out about his award the next morning from the newspapers.

That Sayers, he said, shaking his thin head in mock disbelief, *he is something else. It's good I wasn't there. I would have been a slobbering mess.* But when Gale called, Pic told him,

Magic . . . if you were here now, I'd kiss you.

"In that case," said Gale, "Linda and I will be

over tomorrow. Give you a chance to cool off."

The following day was just as blue and golden as the last. That whole final week of May was glorious as dozens of Brian's friends dropped by to be cheered, to be reassured by the man himself that Pic would be all right. Later, several of the people who saw Brian that week said that they knew—and they felt *he* knew—it would be for the last time.

Brian enjoyed the peace and beauty of his home so much that twice he delayed the trip to Atlanta. Probably his instincts told him the ordeal would be too much. Perhaps he was afraid to see his little princesses or to have them see him.

On May 31st the Piccolos drove out to O'Hare Field and boarded a jet for Atlanta. It was a rough flight. They arrived, to be swarmed upon by Lori, Traci, and Kristi—who found it hard to understand why their daddy didn't fling them about and tease them as usual. Still, Brian refused a wheelchair and walked the long passage from the terminal to the car. By the time they arrived at the Murraths', the ache that had persisted in his chest had turned to severe pain. His cough had become unbearable. (The doctors explained that the cough was caused by the irradiation of the iodine seeds implanted during the pneumonectomy.)

There was a lot of love at the Murraths' that week—and a lot of fear. Joy's younger brother, Herb, Jr., came by. He and Brian had become close friends since the days in Fort Lauderdale when Brian used to promise little Herbie he'd get rides on his motorcycle if Herbie would report on any and all of Joy's male callers. Brian was too ill to continue his old habit of tucking Carol into her four-poster and reviewing the events of the day, as he used to on his other visits. Still, he was not too sick to tease her about the perfume and nightie she had received from one of the boys in her class. At age 20, Carol was graduating from the cerebral palsy school. Brian pretended shock that a boy would send his little sister such a sexy gift. Carol loved it.

But Brian's illness finally overcame his will. Joy was forced to call Dr. Beattie. The doctor suggested they return immediately to New York.

There was one thing Brian wanted before he left. He wondered if it would be possible for Monsignor Regan, the priest who had married Brian and Joy, to give him Holy Communion. It was.

Grace set up a small altar in the bedroom, and his three little girls sat around Brian on the bed. They were very still throughout the ceremony. Communion had never meant so much to the four adults. It was good to be together. As the priest prepared to leave, Brian called after him,

Father, keep praying to your Boss for me.

ADMISSION DATE: 6/4/70   PICCOLO, Brian
                              HOSPITAL #61-54-12
This 26 year old football player was admitted to Memorial Hospital for the fourth time for reevaluation and restart of chemotherapy....

. . . . At the time of admission he was acutely and chronically ill and had lost a great deal of weight. His temperature was 98.4; pulse 108; respirations 24; weight 153½ lbs. Blood pressure 98/50. The left axilla showed the previous operative scar but no recurrence of tumor. There was a fullness over the left lower chest wall consistent with tumor invading the chest wall. There was a dullness throughout the left chest consistent with the left pneumonectomy. The subcutaneous nodule in the region of the xiphoid was smaller. The sternal splitting incision was well healed. His liver and spleen were not palpable. The rest of the examination was unremarkable. . . .

It was the same thing at La Guardia: Brian refused a wheelchair. He was in an agony of pain and fear. The plane trip had been a dull nightmare. He did not notice that New York was beautiful on this early summer Thursday. For Piccolo, New York was never beautiful. It was with relief that he climbed into his bed on the 10th floor at Memorial. They gave him something for the pain and the cough. This time he would have admitted that he was back where he belonged: with the sick people.

Friday they started the torture routine again—tests. Hours out of his bed, being wheeled, poked, turned, punctured, manipulated. Dozens of doctors, nurses, and technicians. And nobody told Brian anything. They said, in fact, "Everything is just fine." He knew nothing was "just fine," but Brian was afraid to ask, afraid to say right out,

"Tell me everything—lay it on the line." The night-time was terrible.

Joy had called Tucker Friday afternoon and asked if he would, again, mind loaning Brian his color television set. Tucker promised to bring it the next morning, and he arrived at the hospital early Saturday, meeting Joy downstairs. They went up together and were alarmed to find the nurses giving Brian oxygen. But it wasn't serious, at least not relatively. Brian was having a little trouble breathing, because of the cough. Tucker didn't stay long. Saturday was a painful, uneventful day. The doctors had not yet announced their latest strategy.

Joy was up at 7:00 A.M. Sunday morning, June 7th, and was walking down First Avenue toward the hospital when she ran into another early riser, Dr. Beattie. She hadn't seen him since their return, and it was such a relief to see his sure, fatherly figure approaching. He already had his arm around her shoulders when she noticed that his eyes didn't have their usual sparkle. "Brian is not doing well at all," he said quietly. "He has a little hepatitis, and also a little cancer in his liver. There were cold spots on the liver scan, and the liver functions tests were not normal." Joy felt her knees buckle. She spoke to Dr. Beattie a few more minutes and walked to St. Catherine's Church, as had become her daily habit. She calmed herself before going up to see Brian.

Brian was restless, but he was asleep. So Joy returned to St. Catherine's for nine o'clock mass.

The rest of the day and Monday and Tuesday were frightening. Brian's chest began to swell around the old scars. The cough, which was not painful, bothered him more than anything, because it kept him from talking. Brian became nervous. The more attention he got, the more his apprehension grew. In retrospect, Joy felt that she and Brian should have been told more about the realities of his condition. And yet, she had never asked.

It's not like in the movies, the doctors say. People victimized by catastrophic disease rarely ask if and when they are going to die. Every doctor has his own way of handling such a patient and his family, but Dr. Beattie takes the positive approach, always. "Aggressive optimism," he calls it. "But never lie to a patient. It's like football, you don't give up until the last whistle." In Brian and Joy, he found two people who, at least consciously, played it his way.

Joy walked into Brian's room on Thursday and found him violently restless with pain. He was on his hands and knees, rocking back and forth, pounding his head on the head of the bed. Joy called for more medicine, and the shot relaxed him. That night she left the hospital early. Tomorrow she was to move into a vacationing doctor's apartment across 67th Street in the Winston, and she had to pack.

Friday morning, for the first time in days, Joy was away from a telephone as she moved her things from one apartment to another. When she got to the hospital, she was told immediately that Dr. Beattie was looking for her. In a panic she ran to Brian's room. She was asked to remain in the hall as the doctors moved in and out. Brian was in shock. The intravenous feeding was infiltrating. Joy waited outside the room for two hours.

Finally, Beattie's chief assistant, Dr. Michael Small, came out. He explained, carefully, everything that was being done. Brian was getting normal white cells, the part of the blood that carries immunities, because by now he was not even immune to mumps. Dr. Small felt that the pain was caused by the tumor in the chest: It was cutting off the blood supply to the left side. Edema had started. They had done a cutdown, gone into the neck to reach the big veins for the IVs. "There is evidence of cancer in the liver, as you know," Dr. Small said. "I don't think Brian is going to live very long."

And *that* was the moment—no sooner—that Joy finally realized Brian was going to die. At some time on Friday she began to make calls to the family. Brian slept all afternoon. He did wake up once: He told Joy to go get something to eat.

Dorothy Kendrick was waiting at the new apartment on Friday night when Joy came in. Joy told Dorothy that she knew Brian was going to die. They talked for a minute or two, and Joy begged Dorothy not to leave her. She had a terrible fear of the telephone. Then she went to bed. One thing Joy had going for her was that she could always sleep; she didn't eat, but she slept soundly.

Dorothy felt that perhaps Joy was hiding, and she was thankful that her tiny friend had at least one refuge.

The apartment on the second floor was small and narrow. Across the street and up to the 10th floor of Memorial, Dorothy could see the light in Brian's room and sometimes shadows moving across the window. She couldn't close her eyes. She was unable to keep them from Brian's window, and no matter where she went in the room, there were eyes on her. The apartment's vacationing owner had a huge stuffed ram with curly horns and, Dorothy swore, human eyes. Dorothy stood guard all that treacherous night, facing the hospital, with her hand on the telephone and the ram's eyes cutting through her back.

The Joseph Piccolos arrived at midnight Friday and saw their son on Saturday morning. Brian's big brother Joe came in from Washington, and his brother Don was there too. Joy tried very hard to prepare them all for the shock of seeing Brian. Joe, Sr., and Irene barely made it through the visit. Joy's brother Herbie arrived and said Herb, Sr., would be there as soon as he delivered Carol to relatives.

All over the country Brian's friends and teammates were waiting. Kathy Kurek was hanging onto her phone in Deerfield. When young Herb called her to say the end was near, she informed Ed McCaskey. Ed began to make arrangements to go by train to New York. He would have been there sooner, but he had been in the hospital with a serious ear infection, and his doctor would not allow him to fly.

In Omaha, Gale was watching over his parents in a hospital. They had been in an automobile accident, and his father was still in a coma. Sunday morning Gale returned to Chicago with a raging fever. By Sunday evening he was in the hospital with a severe infection. It was as if a small part of the world was falling apart.

On Saturday, Brian had been given a transfusion from a man in New Jersey who had been cured of embryonal cell carcinoma six years before. Dr. H. F. Oettgen, the immuno-therapist, was careful to explain that the move was purely experimental, that there was no reason to hope. Joy did not hesitate to give Dr. Oettgen the permission he needed.

Fear was everywhere Sunday—in Joy's voice, in her heart, and in Brian's eyes. He knew his father was scared spitless of flying, and yet here was old Joe hesitantly peering into his room. The flow of medical personnel was increasing steadily. And Brian began to notice the smell.

Joy! he shouted once, *I smell something terrible in here!*

"It must be your breath, Brian. You haven't brushed your teeth in days." Joy made quite a ritual of cleaning his mouth. Brian, when he was awake now, spoke only of petty things.

When she wasn't in her husband's room, Joy sat in a small wooden chair in the lounge at the end of the hall. That's where she was when her father walked in. What a comfort it was to see him! And Brian smiled when Herb entered his room. Pic wasn't the "good lookin' stud" he once loved to be, but he never lost his grin.

At 6:30 P.M. on Sunday, Dr. Beattie gathered the families for a briefing. He sat everyone down in his office and very carefully explained the nature of Brian's disease, and he catalogued every step that he and his staff had taken to stem its rampage. Finally, his voice breaking, he said, "We have failed." Joy went up to the doctor as her father cleared the room. She put her thin arms around him and told him how much she appreciated what he had done, that she knew how hard he had tried. They were quiet for a moment, and then Joy said, "But he has three such beautiful children." "Yes," Ted Beattie answered, "and now you will have to take care of them."

Joy and Dorothy and Herb arrived at the hospital at around eight o'clock on Monday morning. The Piccolos came a bit later. There was more than the usual morning bustle on the 10th floor. Herb and Dorothy stationed themselves again at the end of the hall, wondering, perhaps, how many more hours the vigil could last. Dorothy was relieved when Joy sent her out for some panty hose and a purse. It was good to know what you could do to help. It was good to move.

Joy stayed with Brian, leaving his room only rarely, and then for a sip of Coke or for a breath of fresh air. Monday, June 15th, was the last day Joy Piccolo spent with her husband.

"In the afternoon, Brian was very alert. '*I feel good,*' he said, '*much better.*' All day Monday, which wasn't like Brian, he kept telling me he loved me. I could remember times when I used to yell at him to say 'I love you.' '*If you don't know it by now, forget it,*' he'd say. He always used to tell me he didn't believe in 'love in public.'

"I sat by the bed and laid my head on the pillow where his left arm was elevated to relieve the swelling. All the doctors and nurses and IV equipment were on the right. He would grab for me and shake me and then say, '*I love you.*' The last time, I started to cry, and he said, '*Why are you crying?*' I couldn't help myself. I said, 'Brian, I'm so tired of you being sick. I want to go home.' He said, '*Don't worry, we're going to get out of here. Stop crying, and get yourself something to eat.*'

"I was scared to stay but I didn't want to leave him. I kept wondering what was going through Brian's mind. Did he know he was dying?

"Then Ed walked down the hall. I didn't know who'd called for him, but it was great to see him. Ed had always been there. I knew Brian would be glad to see him, so I went down and shook him awake and told him, 'A big surprise! Someone you'll love to see.' And then there was that big grin again on Brian's face, and tears. Ed automatically stuck out his hand and Brian kept patting it with his swollen arm saying, *'Big Ed . . . Big Ed.'* I thought Ed was going to choke because he hadn't seen Brian like this, either.

"All day Monday he fought off the drugs. He had dreams, but he never lost touch with reality. He kept trying to tell me things. Once he woke up and said, *'Who won the Western Open?'* I said, 'I don't know, Brian.' He was mad. He told me I was supposed to watch it on television. So I left the room and found out that Hugh Royer won and came back and told him. Once he woke up and wanted to know who Ray Nitschke's wife was! I said, 'I don't know, Brian. We didn't meet her in Phoenix. We met him, but not her . . .' Then he dreamt that he saw Kathy Gannon, a girl who went to high school with us and then became a nun. We had seen Kathy on our last visit to Florida, and she had let Lori and Traci wear her veil. He saw another girl too who went to high school with us, Pat Nickle, and he said, *'Funny, why would I be dreaming about them?'*

"Then he woke up and wanted to know the money in the Western Open! I said, 'Brian, I don't know.' *'It is important,'* he told me. *'It is important to know the prize money.'* So I went out and asked Ed, and Ed told me to tell Brian to mind his own business.

"By the time Ed had come, everybody had

had a good cry. There was a little lady who worked in the kitchen. Brian had always called her 'Sexy', because she loved his legs. He used to strut around the halls in his Bermuda pajamas. People just seemed personally involved in what was happening to us. And the family portrait came that day, the one I had been waiting for. Of course, everybody saw it. I didn't know whether to show it to Brian, but I did tell him the picture had arrived, and later he asked to see it. He held the picture up and pointed to the girls and laughed, especially at Lori, his little princess, who was playing shy. And still, he kept saying he loved me.

"Late in the afternoon Brian began to get cramps. A patient in shock perspires a lot and is cool and clammy to the touch. The odor by now was so strong that when anyone opened the door it filled the hallway. Around dinnertime he turned cold, so cold and wet. I got scared. The nurse on duty was the efficient kind, regular army type. I said I wanted to see Dr. Beattie or Dr. Small. She told me I had no reason to call them, nothing had changed. She was right. The blood pressure was the same. I insisted, so she had them paged.

"Dr. Small came in, dressed, as he often was, in slacks and an old sweater. I guess we felt close to him because he was casual, and a little younger than most of the doctors.

He was always honest. He motioned me outside and asked what was the matter. I said, 'I'm scared, Dr. Small. I know it's coming, and I don't know what to do when it comes.' He said, 'I expect you to be scared. It won't be long. I'm afraid he is as bad as he looks. Maybe you ought to go out and get a beer.' That was Dr. Small for you!

"Then he put his arm around me. Dr. Beattie used to hug me all the time; but when Dr. Small got the impulse, I knew we were in trouble. I had a good cry, and then went back.

"As I walked in, Brian called out sharply, *'Joy! Can you believe it? I've got to get to the side of the bed. I've got to dangle.'* He was struggling. I said, 'Honey, you can't dangle, you'll fall out of bed.' *'Oh, no,'* he said, *'I'll feel better.'*

"I called for Ed, and he flew down the hall. 'Take it easy, Pic,' he said, and Brian lay back. 'Joy,' Brian kept saying, *'Can you believe it? I'm going to lick this. I'm going to get out of here,'* and he'd make the okay sign, circling his thumb and forefinger. And he'd relax for awhile.

"Then all of a sudden he sat straight up, with all the tubes hanging and his eyes so big, and he screamed, *'Can you believe it, Joy? Can you believe this shit!'*

"Finally Dr. Beattie came in and examined Brian. He sat down on the couch in the hall with me, and he said it was going to be very soon. I wanted Brian to go to sleep and be comfortable. I didn't want him to be like that for days. So Dr. Beattie said they would give Brian some medication and he would sleep.

"Dr. Beattie was crying when he went down the hall. I sat there beside Brian, knowing that any words were going to be the final words. But there were no more. I went down the hall to tell the others that Brian was going to sleep, that he wouldn't be suffering anymore.

"That was about eleven. The hours seemed to go fast. Everyone was restless, moving. I stayed with Brian. The nurse was in every fifteen minutes, reading the blood and venous pressure. Things kept running through my mind. I'd go out. Ed had some Italian soup for me, but I couldn't eat . . . I was so scared.

"Around midnight Brian began breathing with more difficulty. His mouth and eyes were open. There would be a breath, a huge gasp, and then a sigh. I would make the breath for him. I kept thinking there might not be another, and at every sigh my heart would go down again.

"At about two in the morning I walked out of the room down to the end of the hall and sat with my father. I started crying, from fear, knowing that Brian was never going to talk to me again. Ed came into the lounge and said, 'Brian's nurse wants you.' I started to shake. I walked down the hall; Ed walked with me. I started to cry again before we got to the room, and Ed said, 'Remember, honey, you can't cry, it's a league rule.' So I went in, and Brian was dead.

"He just wasn't suffering anymore."

FINAL DIAGNOSIS:
Malignant teratoma with metastases of embryonal cell carcinoma in left chest, left chest wall, mediastinum, heart, and liver.

I feel very bad about Brian"s death
because I loved him very much. He was
always good to me. Brian would take time
to do things with me. Brian and Joy
would take me to the movies each time we
were together. He would set aside a
special time for us to do something.
Brian would talk over things with me
that I couldn"t understand before bed at
night. I use to tease Brian about being
my number one boyfriemd. I sent him a
lots of names of my boyfriends all the
time. We always tease each other. I
loved going to Chicago. Brian alwasys
had so many things for us to do. The
day Brian gave Joy her engagement ring,
He gave me a ring too. He alaways
makemade feel Part of things. I would
always receive a card from him whenever
they played out of town. He would tell
me about the city or town he was in and
what he thought about the place. Brian
was very sweet to all my friends at the
Cerebral Palsy Center. One of the girls
in my class who cannot talk typed a note
saying that when her sister married she
hoped he would be someone kmk like
Brian. Everytime we went to a football
game, Brian would make sure I had a
special place andx that it was easy for
us to get there with the wheel chair.
When I xxx Visited in Chicago, Whenever
possible he would introduce me to some
of the players on the team. I have lost
a very good friend and I will always
miss him. I loved him so much.

                    Carol Murrath

Brian and I had such a short time together after our marriage, and we were so overwhelmed with football and the babies coming that sometimes I feel I was cheated.

But I know I was also very lucky. I knew my husband was special to me but it wasn't until after his death that I began to realize fully that he had great dimension, despite his youth.

He must have had fears—we all do. But he didn't burden anyone—not even me—not even during his terrible illness. Not once did Brian let up in his fight against cancer. Not once did he acknowledge the possibility of defeat.

My Brian was such a participant in life, every ounce and phase of it. He would make the most ordinary things special. Just taking Lori, Traci, and Kristi to buy shoes was an event, a chance to laugh and play.

Because Brian was self-reliant and willing to make all of our decisions, I depended on him greatly. Now I must learn from him. And I think I'm making progress. Brian believed in himself. He knew he could make things happen. He had no conceit, but he was brazen in his self-confidence.

If someone gives you a compliment, he used to tell me, *say 'thank you'—don't pretend modesty. If you know you can do something, do it.*

Now when our attorney, Irwin Jann, calls and tells me about some sticky legal or financial thing I have to take care of and he says, "Do you think you can handle it?" I tell him, "Don't worry Irwin, I'll be great."

Joy Piccolo
August, 1970

Pro football is not easy—it's a damn tough profession. I think anybody who says it's easy is kidding himself. Sure we're doing something we love. But there's so damn much practice. Hockey, baseball, and basketball players—when they hit their season, they're playing games. We live from week to week—getting ready, always getting ready. It's hard work involving great physical and mental strain. . . but to me, it's a glorious way to make a buck.

You know, it's the fans who make it really worthwhile. You should see the mail I've been getting. I love the notes from kids, things like, "I'm sorry to hear you have a sore chest. Hope it'll get better soon"—things like that. Or the letters from people who have had surgery similar to mine.

Those I really appreciate—especially the ones who've been around awhile after their operations.

I feel I can do a heck of a lot of good, once this thing is licked, but I know it's going to take time. It's not an easy fight, and it's not a short fight. It'll take time—but hell, I've got lots of time.

Brian Piccolo
May, 1970

Any readers who would like to make
a contribution to cancer research
in Brian Piccolo's name can do so by
sending a check to:
The Brian Piccolo
Cancer Research Foundation
Memorial Sloan-Kettering Cancer Center
444 East 68th Street
New York, New York 10021

INDEX